A HOUSE DIVIDING

The Lincoln–Douglas Debates of 1858

✳

A House Dividing

The Lincoln–Douglas
Debates of 1858

STEPHEN BERRY

NEW YORK | OXFORD
Oxford University Press

Oxford University Press is a department of the University of Oxford.
It furthers the University's objective of excellence in research,
scholarship, and education by publishing worldwide.

Oxford   New York
Auckland   Cape Town   Dar es Salaam   Hong Kong   Karachi
Kuala Lumpur   Madrid   Melbourne   Mexico City   Nairobi
New Delhi   Shanghai   Taipei   Toronto

With offices in
Argentina   Austria   Brazil   Chile   Czech Republic   France   Greece
Guatemala   Hungary   Italy   Japan   Poland   Portugal   Singapore
South Korea   Switzerland   Thailand   Turkey   Ukraine   Vietnam

For titles covered by Section 112 of the US Higher Education
Opportunity Act, please visit www.oup.com/us/he for the
latest information about pricing and alternate formats.

Published by Oxford University Press
198 Madison Avenue, New York, New York 10016
http://www.oup.com

Library of Congress Cataloging-in-Publication Data
Berry, Stephen William.
   A house dividing : the Lincoln-Douglas debates of 1858 / Stephen Berry.
      pages cm. -- (Dialogues in history)
   Includes bibliographical references and index.
   ISBN 978-0-19-938996-4 (pbk.)
   1. Lincoln-Douglas Debates, Ill., 1858. 2. Lincoln, Abraham, 1809–1865--Political
career before 1861. 3. Lincoln, Abraham, 1809–1865--Political and social views.
4. Douglas, Stephen A. (Stephen Arnold), 1813–1861--Political and social views.
5. United States--Politics and government--1857–1861. I. Title.
   E457.4.B44 2015
   973.7092--dc23

                                                                 2015008199

Printing Number: 9 8 7 6 5 4 3 2

Printed in the United States of America
on acid-free paper

Table of Contents

Editors' Preface

THE LINCOLN–DOUGLAS DEBATES are widely credited for giving us the modern presidential debate format, although today's candidates have more opportunities for give and take. A typical structure, for instance, has a candidate speaking for two minutes, followed by a ninety-second rebuttal from the opponent and a thirty-second response to the rebuttal from the original speaker. This follows the logic but not the precise timing of the structure Lincoln and Douglas agreed on: one hour for the first candidate, an hour-and-a-half rebuttal from the second, and a thirty-minute rejoinder from the original speaker.

The format of Oxford's "Dialogues" series gives us an extraordinary opportunity to update the Lincoln–Douglas debates for the sound-bite era. Instead of 100,000 words, we have given readers 30,000. Instead of long, uncontested ramblings, we have given them rapid-fire accusations and responses—because despite their reputations as intellectual heavyweights, Lincoln and Douglas were not above mudslinging. Indeed, when disciplined to the modern format, the Lincoln–Douglas debates prove surprisingly studded with ad hominem attacks, political grandstanding, and gross appeals to the candidates' respective bases.

Nor is this the only thing that makes the debates seem modern. The plantation system was a billion-dollar interest that was bad for America. Like any big interest, it warped American politics to protect itself, creating a powerful set of lawyers, lobbyists, preachers, and pols who shilled for it tirelessly. To Douglas, this was simply democracy and capitalism at work; slavery was a legal system, and people had a right to profit from it. This system, moreover, had transformed America into one of the mightiest empires on the globe. To Lincoln, however, some goods and services should not be bought or sold for profit, and we "blow out the moral lights around us" when we think of democracy solely as the implementation of the majority will. Democracy also involves, and perhaps especially involves, the protection and extension of *everyone's* right to life, liberty, and the pursuit of happiness.

The debates that follow are heavily edited, although the edits have been made according to a careful set of rules. Excisions and rearrangements have been made silently and without the use of ellipses. However, no man's meaning was altered thereby; material was never moved from one debate to another; the first and last speaker at the debate were always allowed to have the first and last word here; any words that were inserted (solely for clarity) were set off with square brackets; and the speakers have proportionally the same "air time" here as they did in the 1858 debates.

There may be those who argue that such changes do a kind of violence to the original. The editor would agree, but only if someone is somehow under the impression that this *is* the original. Rod Davis and Doug Wilson have already given us a fantastic ur-text of the debates, published in their Lincoln Studies Center series at Illinois University Press in 2008, and as the historian Allen Guelzo notes on the cover, "no one with even a passing interest in the history of American politics can afford not to read this book." Readers who want a full account of the wider context for the debates and the canvass in which they occurred can do no better than Guelzo's own *Lincoln and Douglas: The Debates That Defined America* (Simon & Schuster, 2008).

A House Dividing is a different exercise—a version of the debates, true to the original, but more available to us in our time. Obviously such a version has limitations, and not merely as an authoritative historical source. The drama plays out differently when the speakers tangle more. But the editor makes no claim that this is exactly how it happened, and he believes that contemporary readers, in a post-modern age, can tell the difference between an authoritative historical text and a bit of educational fun. And any attempt to conflate them, as Lincoln would say, is "but a specious and fantastic arrangement of words, by which a man can prove a horse-chestnut to be a chestnut horse."

The trickiest thing about editing these debates was not only the depth of the cuts (up to eighty percent in some cases) but a very real desire to ensure that the result captured not only the essence of both men's arguments as they evolved over time, but also both men's occasional windbaggery, pettiness, repetitiveness, and moments when they got lost in the political weeds. This too was an essential part of the drama, and rather than cutting it out, it remains in representative samples. Included too are the crowd's comments as recorded by both the pro-Douglas press and the pro-Lincoln press. The result is a quite palpable sense of the *public* nature of these debates. Although both men were up on stage, the crowd around them was close and hungry to be entertained, forcing them to respond to heckling and running commentary from the boisterous throng.

Acknowledgments

The author is pleased to thank Peter and Williamjames Hull Hoffer for the opportunity to contribute to the series. The folks at Oxford University Press were, as usual, the very model of patience and professionalism in bringing this book together. The outside readers—including Alan C. Downs, Georgia Southern University; Songho Ha, University of Alaska–Anchorage; James McGregor, Northeast Texas Community College; Cheryl A. Wells, University of Wyoming; and those remaining anonymous—saved me from little mistakes while shaping my larger thinking. The book is dedicated to all lovers of Lincoln. Lydia Maria Child had it right when she noted: "With all his deficiencies, it must be admitted that [Lincoln] has grown and considering how slavery had weakened and perverted the moral sense of the whole country, it was great good luck to have the people elect a man who was *willing* to grow."

INTRODUCTION

Debating America

ON JULY 21, 1858, Abraham Lincoln boarded the Illinois Central bound for Chicago. He had been on the Senate campaign trail for only two weeks, but already it was going badly. His decision to follow his Democratic opponent, Stephen A. Douglas, from town to town offering refutations of whatever Douglas had said was making Lincoln look defensive and even ridiculous. Somewhat panicked, Lincoln's political handlers recalled him to Chicago and staged an intervention. Lincoln, they said, needed to change tactics immediately; he needed to get onto the same stage as Douglas, not follow him around like a puppy, and he needed to attack more and defend less.

When Lincoln heard the new strategy, he hated it. Douglas was by far the more seasoned debater and was much better known. Any joint appearance would be packed with Douglas partisans and, playing to a Douglas crowd, Lincoln feared he would be shouted down and ridiculed. He was too weak a candidate to dictate strategy, however. His handlers had spoken and he would have to obey.

For his part, Douglas also hated the idea of sharing a stage with Lincoln. "Lincoln is . . . comparatively unknown," Douglas said, whereas "the whole country knows me." On the same rostrum they would look like equals, and if by some miracle Lincoln landed some lucky blows, he would get outsized attention. Better to leave him trailing behind like a puppy.[1]

In the end, Douglas yielded as well. A small man who had never shrunk from a fight, he may have been lured by his love of political combat. Certainly he resented the implication circulating in the opposition press that his refusal would amount to "show[ing] the white feather."[2]

Douglas was precise about his terms: he would not deviate from the schedule of campaign stops he had already organized, but he would agree to meet Lincoln one time each in each of Illinois's nine congressional districts. Because both men had already appeared in the Second and Sixth Districts (Chicago and Springfield) during Lincoln's failed "trail behind" tour, Douglas eliminated those. But he was

The Political Geography of Illinois

Having already spoken in two of Illinois's nine Congressional districts, Lincoln and Douglas agreed to hold joint debates in the remaining seven.

willing to meet Lincoln in the seven remaining districts, at Ottawa (in the Third District) on August 21; at Freeport (First District) on August 27; at Jonesboro (Ninth District) on September 15; at Charleston (Seventh District) on September 18; at Galesburg (Fourth District) on October 7; at Quincy (Fifth District) on October 13; and at Alton (Eighth District) on October 15. The format would be simple: Douglas would open the first debate and speak for an hour; Lincoln could then speak for ninety minutes, and Douglas would close with a thirty-minute rebuttal. This format would be repeated in all the debates, but the candidates would alternate who got to lead off. Douglas would thus get the first and last words at the majority of the seven debates (and the first and last words in the debates as a whole), but he made it clear that these were the only terms Lincoln could expect. Again, Lincoln could only agree.

Thus were the two principals dragged into the Lincoln–Douglas debates, one of the more legendary pieces of political theater in the history of the United States. Over two months, at seven stops, Lincoln and Douglas traded blows on the thorniest issue of the day—whether the institution of slavery could and should expand into the territories—and the nation hung on every word, thanks in part to a pool of stenographers and a recently formed telegraphic news service called the Associated Press.

The Undecided Political Prize Fight
In the antebellum period, politics was often compared with other combative, spectator sports, especially boxing. Here the man in Lincoln's corner is African American, signifying Lincoln's support among abolitionists. The man in Douglas's corner is Irish, who typically supported the Democratic Party in the period.

Lincoln and Douglas shared little in common beyond what minimally qualified them to meet on a political stage in Illinois. Both had migrated to the state in their twenties and studied law before getting into politics. (Both had also courted Mary Todd, although her interest in Douglas, and his in her, has been exaggerated. "I liked him well enough," Mary said later, "but that was all.") Ultimately both had also married into slaveholding families, although only Douglas benefited directly and financially, receiving a twenty percent share of the proceeds from his father-in-law's plantation. Beyond this, the men were a study in contrasts, physically, politically, and psychologically. Douglas was affectionately known as "The Little Giant"—a five-foot-four "steam engine in breeches" with legs so short fellow politician Thomas Hart Benton complained that "that part of his body . . . which men wish to kick, is too near the ground!" With a sharp eye for fashion, Douglas dressed "plantation style" in ruffled shirts, richly colored coats, and broad-brimmed felt hats. At six-foot-four, Lincoln by unfortunate contrast was "thin as a bean pole and ugly as a scarecrow." Careless about his clothes, he had the appearance of a slovenly undertaker. "I have never," said one witness, "seen any other two public men appearing on the same platform so unlike in stature."[3]

Stephen A. Douglas

The political contrasts were sharper. An early admirer of Andrew Jackson, Douglas was a lifelong Democrat. His legislative agenda emphasized geographic expansion, a transcontinental railroad, free land for whites, and a streamlined process for territorial governments to organize. Douglas had supported the annexation of Texas, the acquisition of Oregon (and later Cuba), and the Mexican–American War, in which the United States had seized fifty-five percent of Mexico's territory (this despite the fact that Mexico had been following America's lead in declaring its independence from an Old World colonizer and creating a new republic in the American model). Douglas, however, had no misgivings. "You cannot fix bounds to the onward march of this great and growing country," he said. It was for just such cavalier optimism that Douglas was beloved. His rise in the era's dominant party had been so meteoric, one journalist called it a "run of luck almost without parallel in politics."

Lincoln's political road had been rockier. An early admirer of Jackson's great nemesis, Henry Clay, Lincoln had clung to Clay's Whig Party even after it had died. Where Democrats like Douglas emphasized geographic expansion, the Whigs emphasized economic development, supporting a more diversified, less

Abraham Lincoln

agricultural economy with more libraries and schools, higher protective tariffs for American industry, and greater development of urban infrastructure. As a party, the Whigs succeeded in electing two presidents by, somewhat inconsistently, backing politically unaffiliated war heroes. But as a national politician, Lincoln had stumbled right out of the gate, snuffing out his one-term congressional career with his opposition to the Mexican–American War. (His own constituents dubbed him the "Benedict Arnold of our district" for his claim that the war was unnecessary and unconstitutional.)

Of the two men, then, Douglas seemed more on track, not only to be reelected to the Senate but also to one day become president. "Senator Douglas is of world-wide renown," Lincoln admitted. "All of the anxious [office-seekers] of his party . . . have seen in his jolly, fruitful face, post offices, land offices, marshalships and cabinet appointments, chargeships and foreign missions, bursting and sprouting forth in wonderful exuberance, ready to be laid hold of. . . . On the contrary nobody has ever expected me to be President. In my poor, lean, lank face nobody has [even] seen that cabbages were sprouting out." By 1852, Douglas was a leading candidate for the Democratic presidential nomination; meanwhile, the pulse of Lincoln's political career was so faint, he had returned in earnest to his law practice. Even so, his passion for politics was continuously stoked by the South's growing insistence that the institution of slavery was not a "necessary evil" but a "positive good."[4]

Between 1820 and 1844, white Americans had swept most of the remaining native tribes off of twenty-five million acres of the most valuable farmland in the Old Southwest. There they erected a Cotton Kingdom that would go on to produce seventy percent of the world's cotton supply and catalyze the Western world's early industrialization. The U.S. cotton crop had doubled every decade from 1820 to 1860; 1860's crop was the largest and most profitable on record. And, yes, Northerners made some of the money; but Southerners made more. With only one-third of the country's white population, the South had two-thirds of the men worth more than $100,000, men who would today be millionaires. The "big-bugs" of the South, noted one visitor to Alabama, "live in cotton houses and ride in cotton carriages. They buy cotton, sell cotton, think cotton, eat cotton, drink cotton, and dream cotton. They marry cotton wives, and unto them are born cotton children."[5]

Central to this massive concentration of wealth was the work of enslaved African Americans who endured what historian Ira Berlin has called the "Second Middle Passage"—the forced migration of a million men, women, and children from the older plantation states of the tidewater to the more brutal work regimes of Mississippi, Alabama, Louisiana, and (eventually) Texas. The vast majority of these families were not moved intact. Instead they were broken apart to enter a new industry as commodified human beings—as "prime hands," "bucks," "breeding wenches," and "fancy girls." "The internal slave trade became the largest enterprise in the South outside the plantation itself," historian Ira Berlin has concluded, "and probably the most advanced in its employment of modern transportation, finance, and publicity."[6]

Erecting a cotton kingdom was not something the Founding Fathers had ever envisioned. They had seen slavery as an evil, a relic of barbarism, and an institution at odds with their own Revolutionary legacy, which had struck down tyranny in all its forms. But with so much money to be made, men often find ways to keep the boom times booming, and white Southerners gradually began to argue that the Founding Fathers had been flat wrong. In founding a new government for the deep South in 1861, Confederate vice president Alexander Stephens admitted that "the prevailing ideas entertained by [Jefferson], and most of the leading statesmen at the time of the formation of the old Constitution were, that the enslavement of the African was in violation of the laws of nature; that it was wrong in principle, socially, morally and politically. It was an evil they knew not well how to deal with; but the general opinion of the men of that day was, that, somehow or other, in the order of Providence, the institution would be evanescent and pass away. . . . Those ideas, however, were fundamentally wrong [because] they rested upon the assumption of the equality of races. This was an error. . . . Our new Government is founded upon exactly the opposite ideas; its foundations are laid, its cornerstone rests, upon the great truth that the negro is not equal to the white man; [and] that slavery, subordination to the superior race, is his natural and moral condition."[7]

What had happened? In a single generation, Stephens and a million other Southerners like him had gotten themselves completely turned around. They had turned their backs on Jefferson, the Declaration of Independence, their history, and their own former understanding of slavery as an evil. And they had done it all for cotton. They had done it all for coin.

This, at least, was how Lincoln saw it in 1858 on the eve of the debates. By that time, he and Douglas had been arguing with each other about virtually everything for more than twenty years. Focused on erecting an empire of genuine (white) liberty and (white) opportunity, Douglas did not see the cultural rot Lincoln saw. He saw with great pride an emerging American colossus—a country that had doubled in size twice in a single generation, a country that seemed destined to become the mightiest empire since Rome.

Central to all that expansion and all that success, however, was the enormous profitability of slavery, and by 1858 proslavery forces were on the march. For many Americans, the question of slavery's expansion had been laid to rest in 1820, when the Missouri Compromise dictated that Missouri would be the only slave state carved out of the Louisiana Purchase above the 36' 30° parallel. When it came time to organize those territories, however, proslavery forces insisted that the Missouri Compromise had been unconstitutional and that slavery should be allowed in. As chairman of the Committee on Territories, Stephen Douglas tried to split the difference by suggesting that Congress should not determine the status of territories, slave or free, but rather leave it to the people in those territories to decide for themselves. "It is none of my business which way the slavery clause (in Kansas) is decided," Douglas told the Senate. "I care not whether it is voted down or voted up." This may have been true. Douglas was far more interested in the fact that opening up the territories to settlement of any kind would make a transcontinental railroad (preferably from Chicago to San Francisco) financially viable. Unfortunately his "popular sovereignty" doctrine did not solve but rather aggravated the question of slavery in the territories. In effectively nullifying the Missouri Compromise, Douglas divided his own Democratic party and created open warfare between proslavery and antislavery settlers in Kansas.

In 1856, proslavery forces scored another victory with the election of Pennsylvania Democrat James Buchanan, who rode into office with the support of fourteen of the fifteen slave states (carrying only four of the fourteen northern states). Buchanan rewarded the South's loyalty with key cabinet posts, including secretary of the Treasury, Howell Cobb (Georgia), secretary of the Interior, Jacob Thompson (Mississippi), and secretary of war, John Floyd (Virginia), not to mention his vice

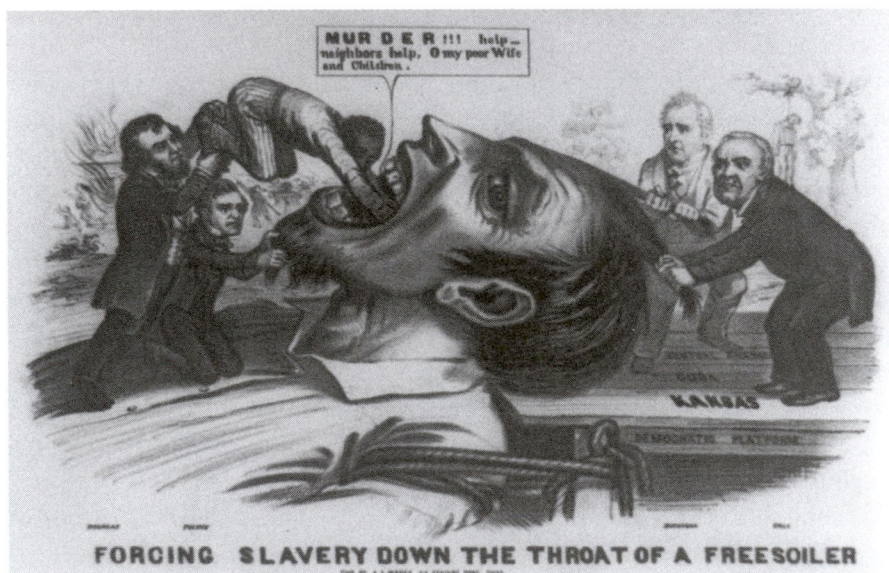

Forcing Slavery down the Throat of a Freesoiler
Lilliputian proslavery forces are stuffing the institution of slavery down America's throat.
The small figures at the left are Stephen A. Douglas and sitting president Franklin Pierce.
(The figures at the right are Democratic presidential nominee James Buchanan and
Democratic senator Lewis Cass.) In the background are images that suggest the violence
and mayhem the proslavery forces are causing. The territorial ambitions of the slavocracy
are symbolized by the planks in the "Democratic Platform."

president, John C. Breckinridge (Kentucky). Buchanan also went before Congress to support Kansas coming into the Union as a slave state under the Lecompton Constitution, a fraudulent document drawn up by the state's minority of slaveholders.

Proslavery forces scored their greatest victory, however, when two days after Buchanan's inauguration, and partly as a result of his finagling, the Supreme Court handed down its decision in *Dred Scott v. Sandford*. With the help of abolitionist lawyers, the slave Scott had sued for freedom in a Missouri court on the basis that he had been taken into free states and territories by his former master, a U.S. Army surgeon. Writing for the majority, Chief Justice Roger B. Taney determined not only that Scott remained a slave but also that Congress had had no right to determine the status, free or slave, of the area Scott had sojourned in, territories that made up the Louisiana Purchase, and that the Missouri Compromise was therefore unconstitutional. This was a direct challenge to the raison d'etre of the Republican Party, which held that Congress *did* have the power to regulate slavery in the territories and thereby create free states. Moreover, the end logic of the *Scott* decision was that slaves were like any other form of property and could be taken anywhere in the country. To many Republicans, including Lincoln, this string of proslavery successes all pointed toward one thing—a concerted effort to *nationalize* the institution of slavery and destroy the very concept of a "free state." "The conspiracy is nearly completed," announced the *Albany Evening Journal*. "The Legislation of the Republic is in the hands of [a] handful of Slaveholders."[8]

To Lincoln, the fault for all this lay less with the slavocracy (moneyed interests were just doing what moneyed interests do) than with its sycophants and enablers. And Douglas was the worst enabler of all because he carried such a seductive message. America could and should just keep growing, Douglas said; we owe it to ourselves, to our posterity, and to all mankind. Lincoln had faced this argument before in standing up to the Mexican War—and had suffered the consequences. Under other circumstances, he could have liked Douglas. Certainly Douglas liked him. When, much later, he received the telegram that Lincoln had been nominated to run against him as president, Douglas turned to two Republicans and said, "Well, gentlemen, you have nominated a very able and a very honest man." Lincoln was less forgiving. He had a particular distaste for the men who, however unwittingly, shilled for the Slave Power, and he found Douglas too typical of the politicians who demonstrated a "want . . . of rectitude" and "lack of . . . morals"—qualities forgivable in an individual but deeply dangerous to the republic. Illinois state senator Joseph Gillespie perhaps best captured this contrast between the two men when he said, "Douglas headed a party. Lincoln stood upon a principle."[9]

The two men also had different rhetorical styles. Douglas's definitive biographer, Robert Johannsen, concluded that Douglas "was a pragmatic, professional politician, frequently bumptious and full of bluster, subject to outbursts of oratory that were not always designed to clarify the issues under discussion." Even so, Douglas was a political dynamo who lived for the stage, and he served up the kind of richly brocaded paeans to America that Americans loved to hear. A rich basso profondo with a voice "like the roar of a lion," Douglas "had a 'magnetism' about him almost irresistible," noted one witness. Another New England reporter thought him the oratorical equivalent of a prizefighter with all his "pluck, quickness and strength; adroitness in shifting his positions, avoiding his adversary's blows, and hitting him in unexpected places in return." Douglas was also the more disciplined debater, never straying far from his main talking points.[10]

As a speaker, Lincoln had a different kind of magnetism. A shrill tenor, his voice was almost as unprepossessing as his face, and audiences often had to adjust to the aural unpleasantness of hearing him speak. Gradually they would, however, and an argument Lincoln might have lost in five minutes he tended to win in fifty as the force of his logic began to accumulate. Lincoln is remembered as a beautiful writer, with a flair for what he called the "lilt of the language." This is true, but in the Lincoln–Douglas debates it was more often Douglas who waxed poetic. Lincoln comes across more as a relentless logician, undoubtedly the result of having spent a lifetime before the bar. As a lawyer, Lincoln hated what he called "surplusage" or "dead wood"; he wanted people to dig down quickly to "hard pan." "He was terribly impatient," remembered one fellow circuit-rider, "if any lawyer, in arguing a case, 'beat around the bush' or talked 'wide of the mark.'" He would "go mad almost," remembered another, "at [any]one who couldn't explain plainly what he wanted to convey." Asked to put his finger on what made Lincoln such a successful speaker, an acquaintance noted, "because when he was asked a question and gave an answer it was always characteristic, brief, pointed, *a propos*, out of the common way and manner, and yet *exactly* suited to the time, place and thing."[11]

What was at stake in the debates, however, was more than the reputations and political fortunes of any two men. The United States was at a crossroads. In two generations, the country had secured and defended its independence in wars with the mightiest nation on earth—Great Britain. It had quadrupled in population and quadrupled in size. From a huddled series of seaboard colonies, America was now an empire, sweeping to the Pacific, seemingly destined to create a civilization that would stand for all time.

And yet the deepening sectional crisis tainted each national success, giving the American project an almost self-defeating aspect. With each new conquest, a manifest destiny that might have been expected to bring national unity brought deeper division. Poised to achieve greatness, America was instead threatened with self-destruction. "Shall we expect some transatlantic military giant, to step the Ocean, and crush us at a blow?" Lincoln had asked in 1838. "Never!—All the armies of Europe, Asia and Africa combined, with all the treasure of the earth (our own excepted) in their military chest; with a Buonaparte for a commander, could not by force, take a drink from the Ohio, or make a track on the Blue Ridge, in a trial of a thousand years. At what point then is the approach of danger to be expected? I answer, if it ever reach us, it must spring up amongst us. It cannot come from

Lincoln on the Rostrum
This artist's rendering of the Lincoln–Douglas debates demonstrates just how close
the speakers were to the crowd.

abroad. If destruction be our lot, we must ourselves be its author and finisher. As a nation of freemen, we must live through all time, or die by suicide."[12]

Lincoln knew his history. Great empires are not conquered. They conquer themselves and rot from within. As Lincoln and Douglas stepped onto the stage, the question, then, was not merely whether the country would "live through all time, or die by suicide" but whether reasonable men could so save the country "as to make, and to keep it, forever worthy of the saving." Douglas was willing to compromise with the Slave Power in part because the alternative, civil war, seemed dreadful to contemplate. Lincoln was not willing to compromise because the alternative, the complete overthrow of American ideals, was more dreadful to contemplate. For Lincoln, America was an idea before it was a country. And when that idea became too compromised, the country was dead already.[13]

✳

The Debates

First Debate, Ottawa, Illinois, August 21, 1858

The first of the seven scheduled Lincoln–Douglas debates took place in the small town of Ottawa, Illinois, in the far north of the state. Situated at the confluence of the Illinois and Fox rivers, Ottawa was connected by rail to Chicago about eighty miles (and four hours) to the east. The debate itself was scheduled for two o'clock on the afternoon of August 21, in Washington Square, Ottawa's town park, where a platform had been erected with an awning to shield the debaters and other dignitaries. Long before then, however, Ottawa's population began to swell with the more than 10,000 spectators who quickly filled up all available homes and hotels and then camped on the river bluffs, their evening fires making "it look," said one witness, "as if an army was gathered about us." The morning of the twenty-first was a dry one, and as the foot and horse traffic increased on the roads into town, a dust cloud was raised until the square "resembled a vast smoke house." Ottawa was the county seat of La Salle, a county that had gone for Republican John C. Fremont in the presidential contest of 1856. Ottawans, then, might naturally have favored Lincoln had they known anything about him. Unfortunately for Lincoln, the only things they really knew they didn't like: Lincoln, they thought, was a "downstater," born in Kentucky and therefore of suspect principles, a man who had served a single ignominious term in Congress more than a decade before and hadn't been much heard from since. "Nobody who was anybody was for Lincoln," remembered one local. Delayed by the traffic on the roads, Lincoln and Douglas did not mount the rostrum until two-thirty. They did not shake hands. "Their demeanor on the platform was that of cool politeness," remembered one witness. "There was nothing like comradeship between them."4

Douglas: *"Ladies and gentlemen: I appear before you today for the purpose of discussing the leading political topics which now agitate the public mind. Prior to 1854 this country was divided into two great political parties, known as the Whig and Democratic parties. Both were national and patriotic, advocating principles that were universal in their application. An old line Whig could*

proclaim his principles in Louisiana and Massachusetts alike. Whig principles had no boundary sectional line, they were not limited by the Ohio river, nor by the Potomac, nor by the line of the free and slave States, but applied and were proclaimed wherever the Constitution ruled or the American flag waved over the American soil. [Cheers.]

While the Whig and Democratic parties differed in regard to a bank, the tariff, distribution, the specie circular and the sub-treasury, they stood on the same platform with regard to the slavery question. That platform was the right of the people of each State and each Territory to decide their local and domestic institutions for themselves, subject only to the federal constitution.

[But] in 1854, Mr. Abraham Lincoln and Mr. [Lyman] Trumbull entered into an arrangement, one with the other, and each with his respective friends, to dissolve the old Whig party on the one hand, and to dissolve the old Democratic party on the other, and to connect the members of both into an Abolition party under the name and disguise of a Republican party. [Laughter, cheers.] Lincoln went to work to abolitionize the Old Whig party all over the State, pretending that he was then as good a Whig as ever [Laughter], and Trumbull went to work in his part of the State, preaching Abolitionism in its milder and lighter form, and trying to abolitionize the Democratic party, and bring old Democrats handcuffed and bound hand and foot into the Abolition camp. [Cheers.]

In contemporary America, politicians who make veiled racist appeals are said to be "blowing the dog whistle." Do you think this is what Douglas is doing when he refers to abolition "in its milder and *lighter* form" [emphasis added] or when he conjures up images of old Democrats being dragged into the Abolition camp "bound hand and foot"?

In pursuance of the arrangement, the parties met at Springfield in October 1854, and proclaimed their new platform. Lincoln was to bring into the Abolition camp the old line Whigs, and transfer them over to Giddings, Chase, Fred Douglass, and Parson Lovejoy, who were ready to receive them and christen them in their new faith. [Laughter, cheers.] They laid down on that occasion a platform for their new Republican party, and I now hold [that platform] in my hands and put the question to Abraham Lincoln this day, whether he now stands and will stand by each article in that creed and carry it out. [Cheers.]

I desire to know whether Mr. Lincoln today stands as he did in 1854, in favor of the unconditional repeal of the Fugitive Slave Law. I desire him to answer whether he stands pledged today, as he did in 1854, against the admission of any more slave States into the Union, even if the people want them. I want to know whether he stands pledged against the admission of a new State into the Union

with such a Constitution as the people of that State may see fit to make.
[Cheers.] I want to know whether he stands today pledged to the abolition of
slavery in the District of Columbia. I desire him to answer whether he stands
pledged to the prohibition of the slave trade between the different States. I desire
to know whether he stands pledged to prohibit slavery in all the territories of the
United States, North as well as South of the Missouri Compromise line. I desire
him to answer whether he is opposed to the acquisition of any more territory
unless slavery is prohibited therein. I want his answer to these questions. I ask
Abraham Lincoln to answer these questions, in order that when I trot him down
to lower Egypt, I may put the same questions to him. [Applause.] My principles
are the same everywhere. [Cheers.] I can proclaim them alike in the North, the
South, the East, and the West. My principles will apply wherever the Constitu-
tion prevails and the American flag waves. [Applause.]

Lincoln: *My fellow citizens: When a man hears himself somewhat misrepre-*
sented, it provokes him. But when misrepresentation becomes very gross and
palpable, it is more apt to amuse him. [Laughter.] This story that Judge
Douglas tells of Trumbull bargaining to sell out the old Democratic party, and
Lincoln agreeing to sell out the old Whig party—I have the means of knowing
about that, [Laughter] and I know there is no substance to it whatever. I hope
you will permit me to read a part of a printed speech that I made at Peoria,
which will show the [actual] position I took in that contest of 1854.

Voice from crowd: *"Put on your specs."*

Lincoln: *"Yes, sir, I am obliged to do so. I am no longer a young man."*
[Laughter.]

Lincoln, reading:

"I hate [slavery] because of the monstrous injustice of slavery itself. I hate it
because it deprives our republican example of its just influence in the world,
enables the enemies of free institutions, with plausibility, to taunt us as hypo-
crites, causes the real friends of freedom to doubt our sincerity, and especially
because it forces so many really good men amongst ourselves into an open war
with the very fundamental principles of civil liberty—criticizing the Declara-
tion of Independence, and insisting that there is no right principle of action
but self-interest.

"When Southern people tell us they are no more responsible for the origin
of slavery than we, I acknowledge the fact. When it is said that the institution
exists, and that it is very difficult to get rid of it, in any satisfactory way, I can
understand and appreciate the saying. I surely will not blame them for not
doing what I should not know how to do myself. If all earthly power were given
me, I should not know what to do, as to the existing institution. My first im-
pulse would be to free all the slaves, and send them to Liberia,—to their own
native land. But a moment's reflection would convince me, that whatever of
high hope there may be in this, in the long run, its sudden execution is impos-
sible. What then? Free them all, and keep them among us as underlings? Is it
quite certain that this betters their condition? I think I would not hold [them]

in slavery at any rate; yet the point is not clear enough to me to denounce people upon. What next? Free them, and make them politically and socially our equals? My own feelings will not admit of this; and if mine would, we well know that those of the great mass of white people will not. Whether this feeling accords with justice and sound judgment, is not the sole question, if, indeed, it is any part of it. A universal feeling, whether well or ill-founded, cannot be safely disregarded. We cannot, then, make them equals. It does seem to me that systems of gradual emancipation might be adopted; but for their tardiness in this, I will not undertake to judge our brethren of the South.

"When they remind us of their constitutional rights, I acknowledge them, not grudgingly, but fully and fairly; and I would give them any legislation for the reclaiming of their fugitives, which should not, in its stringency, be more likely to carry a free man into slavery, than our ordinary criminal laws are to hang an innocent one.

"But all this, to my judgment, furnishes no more excuse for permitting slavery to go into our own free territory, than it would for reviving the African slave-trade by law. The law which forbids the bringing of slaves from Africa, and that which has so long forbid the taking of them to Nebraska, can hardly be distinguished on any moral principle; and the repeal of the former could find quite as plausible excuses as that of the latter."

Now, gentlemen, I don't want to read at any greater length, but this is the true complexion of all I have ever said in regard to the institution of slavery and the black race. This is the whole of it, and anything that argues me into his idea of perfect social and political equality with the negro, is but a specious and fantastic arrangement of words, by which a man can prove a horse-chestnut to be a chestnut horse. [Laughter.]

What do you think of Lincoln's stand on race? How much do you think is driven by the political exigencies of the moment, and how much do you think these sentiments reflect his own views? Why does he say, "my own feelings will not admit of [true racial equality]; and if mine would. . . ."? Does he mean to imply that his own feelings *might* admit of true racial equality? Or is he purposely leaving things vague so he can appeal both to those who do and to those who don't believe in social and legal equality for African Americans?

I will say here, while upon this subject, that I have no purpose, directly or indirectly, to interfere with the institution of slavery in the States where it exists. I believe I have no lawful right to do so, and I have no inclination to do so. I have no purpose to introduce political and social equality between the white

and the black races. There is a physical difference between the two, which, in my judgment, will probably forever forbid their living together upon the footing of perfect equality, and inasmuch as it becomes a necessity that there must be a difference, I, as well as Judge Douglas, am in favor of the race to which I belong having the superior position. I have never said anything to the contrary, but I hold that, notwithstanding all this, there is no reason in the world why the negro is not entitled to all the natural rights enumerated in the Declaration of Independence, the right to life, liberty, and the pursuit of happiness. [Loud cheers.] *I hold that he is as much entitled to these as the white man. I agree with Judge Douglas he is not my equal in many respects—certainly not in color, perhaps not in moral or intellectual endowment. But in the right to eat the bread, without the leave of anybody else, which his own hand earns,* he is my equal and the equal of Judge Douglas, and the equal of every living man. [Great applause.]

   Douglas: *In the remarks I have made on this platform, and the position of Mr. Lincoln upon it, I mean nothing personally disrespectful or unkind to that gentleman. I have known him for nearly twenty-five years. There were many points of sympathy between us when we first got acquainted. We were both comparatively boys, and both struggling with poverty in a strange land. I was a school-teacher in the town of Winchester, and he a flourishing grocery keeper in the town of Salem.* [Applause and laughter.] *He was more successful in his occupation than I was in mine, and hence more fortunate in this world's goods. Lincoln is one of those peculiar men who perform with admirable skill everything which they undertake. I made as good a schoolteacher as I could, and when a cabinet maker I made a good bedstead and tables, although my old boss said I succeeded better with bureaus and secretaries than with anything else;* [Cheers] *but I believe that Lincoln was always more successful in business than I, for his business enabled him to get into the legislature. I met him there, however, and had sympathy with him, because of the up-hill struggle we both had in life. He was then just as good at telling an anecdote as now.* ["No doubt."] *He could beat any of the boys wrestling or running a foot-race, in pitching quoits or tossing a copper; could ruin more liquor than all the boys of the town together,* [uproarious laughter] *and the dignity and impartiality with which he presided at a horse-race or fist-fight excited the admiration and won the praise of everybody that was present and participated.* [Renewed laughter.]

Douglas's portrait of Lincoln's early life and personal habits is grossly inaccurate. Lincoln did not drink, for instance, and Lincoln had been poor in a way that Douglas never was. What do you make of Douglas's portrait of Lincoln's early life? Do you think he knew the truth? What is Douglas hoping to achieve by this depiction?

I sympathized with him, because he was struggling with difficulties, and so was I. Mr. Lincoln served with me in the Legislature in 1836, when we both retired, and he subsided, or became submerged, and he was lost sight of as a public man for some years. In 1846, when Wilmot introduced his celebrated proviso, and the abolition tornado swept over the country, Lincoln again turned up as a member of Congress from the Sangamon district. I was then in the Senate of the United States, and was glad to welcome my old friend and companion. Whilst in Congress, he distinguished himself by his opposition to the Mexican war, taking the side of the common enemy against his own country; ["that's true"] and when he returned home, he found that the indignation of the people followed him everywhere, and he was again submerged or obliged to retire into private life, forgotten by his former friends. ["And will be again."]

In opposing the Mexican War ten years earlier, Lincoln had followed the lead of his "beau ideal of a statesman," Henry Clay, who had come out against "the unnatural war with Mexico" in 1847. Lincoln read Clay's speech on his way to his first (and only) term in Congress and determined to condemn President Polk's unilateral land grab in Mexico. In his maiden speech to Congress, Lincoln said that the war had been (illegally) started by the president and would now have to be seen through by the people, and soldiers should be given every support. But he also demanded to know the exact "spot" on which American blood had been shed on American soil—Polk's claimed pretext for the war. Although Lincoln's speech was no more strident than that of many other Whigs, it was deeply unpopular in Illinois, where more soldiers had been sent to Mexico than from any other state except Missouri. Lincoln would be derided as "spotty Lincoln" and a traitor until his death. Do you think Douglas was right—had Lincoln taken the side of the "enemy against his own country" during the Mexican War? Even if the charge isn't true, is it effective?

He came up again in 1854, just in time to make this abolition or Black Republican platform, in company with Giddings, Lovejoy, Chase and Fred Douglass, for the Republican party to stand upon. [Laughter, "Hit him again," &c.]
   Lincoln: The Judge is woefully at fault about his early friend Lincoln being a "grocery keeper." [Laughter.] I don't know as it would be a great sin, if I had been, but he is mistaken. Lincoln never kept a grocery anywhere in the world. [Laughter.] It is true that Lincoln did work the latter part of one winter in a

little still house, up at the head of a hollow. [Roars of laughter.] And so I think my friend, the Judge, is equally at fault when he charges me at the time when I was in Congress of having opposed our soldiers who were fighting in the Mexican War. The Judge did not make his charge very distinctly, but I can tell you what he can prove, by referring to the record. You remember I was an old Whig, and whenever the Democratic party tried to get me to vote that the war had been righteously begun by the President, I would not do it. But whenever they asked for any money, or land-warrants, or anything to pay the soldiers there, during all that time, I gave the same vote that Judge Douglas did. [Loud applause.]

Douglas: *Let me read a part of [Lincoln's] speech at Springfield to the convention which nominated him for the Senate, he said:*

"In my opinion it will not cease until a crisis shall have been reached and passed. 'A house divided against itself cannot stand.' I believe this government cannot endure permanently half Slave and half Free. I do not expect the Union to be dissolved—I do not expect the house to fall—but I do expect it will cease to be divided. It will become all one thing, or all the other. Either the opponents of slavery will arrest the further spread of it, and place it where the public mind shall rest in the belief that it is in the course of ultimate extinction: or its advocates will push it forward till it shall became alike lawful in all the States—old as well as new—North as well as South."

["Good," "good," and cheers.]

I am delighted to hear you Black Republicans say "good." [Laughter and cheers.] *I have no doubt that doctrine expresses your sentiments* ["Hit them again," "that's it"], *and I will prove to you now, if you will listen to me, that it is revolutionary and destructive of the existence of this government.* ["Hurrah for Douglas," "good," and cheers.] *Mr. Lincoln, in the extract from which I have read, says that this Government cannot endure permanently in the same condition in which it was made by its framers—divided into free and slave states. He says that it has existed for about eighty years thus divided, and yet he tells you that it cannot endure permanently on the same principles and in the same relative condition in which our fathers made it. Why can it not exist divided into free and slave states? Washington, Jefferson, Franklin, Madison, Hamilton, Jay, and the great men of that day, made this government divided into free states and slave states, and left each state perfectly free to do as it pleased on the subject of slavery.* ["Right, right."] *Why can it not exist on the same principles on which our fathers made it?* ["It can."] *Suppose this doctrine of uniformity preached by Mr. Lincoln—that the States should all be free or all be slave—had prevailed. And what would have been the result? Of course, the twelve slaveholding states would have overruled the one free state, and slavery would have been fastened by a constitutional provision on every inch of the American republic, instead of being left as our fathers wisely left it, to each state to decide for itself.* ["Good, good," and three cheers for Douglas.] *Here I assert that uniformity in the local laws and institutions of the different States in neither possible or desirable. If uniformity had been adopted when the government was established, it must inevitably have been the uniformity of slavery everywhere, or else the uniformity of negro citizenship and negro equality everywhere.*

Lincoln: [The Judge] has read from my speech in Springfield in which I say that "a house divided against itself cannot stand." Does the Judge say it can stand? [Laughter.] *I don't know whether he does or not. The Judge does not seem to be attending to me just now, but I would like to know if it is his opinion that a house divided against itself can stand. If he does, then there is a question of veracity, not between him and me, but between the Judge and an authority of a somewhat higher character.* [Laughter and applause.]

Now, my friends, I ask your attention to this matter for the purpose of saying something seriously. I know that the Judge may readily enough agree with me that the maxim which was put forth by the Savior is true, but he may allege that I misapply it. And the Judge has a right to urge that, in my application, I do misapply it, and then I have a right to show that I do not misapply it. When he undertakes to say that because I think this nation, so far as the question of slavery is concerned, will all become one thing or all the other, I am in favor of bringing about a dead uniformity in the various states, in all their institutions, he argues erroneously. The great variety of the local institutions in the states—springing from differences in the soil, differences in the face of the country, and in the climate—are bonds of Union. They do not make a house divided against itself, but they make a house united. If they produce, in one section of the country, what is called for by the wants of another section, and this other section can supply the wants of the first, they are not matters of discord but bonds of union, true bonds of union.

But can this question of slavery be considered as among these varieties in the institutions of the country? I leave it to you to say whether, in the history of our Government, this institution of slavery has not always failed to be a bond of union, and, on the contrary, been an apple of discord and an element of division in the house. [Cries of "Yes, yes," and applause.] *If so, then I have a right to say that, in regard to this question, the Union is a house divided against itself. And when the Judge reminds me that I have often said to him that the institution of slavery has existed for eighty years in some states, and yet it does not exist in some others, I agree to the fact, and I account for it by looking at the position in which our fathers originally placed it—restricting it from the new territories where it had not gone, and legislating to cut off its source by the abrogation of the slave trade, thus putting the seal of legislation against its spread. The public mind did rest in the belief that it was in the course of ultimate extinction.* [Cries of "Yes, yes."] *But lately, I think—and in this I charge nothing on the Judge's motives—lately, I think, that he, and those acting with him, have placed that institution on a new basis, which looks to the perpetuity and nationalization of slavery.* [Loud cheers.] *Now,*

I believe if we could arrest the spread, and place it where Washington and Jefferson and Madison placed it, it would be in the course of ultimate extinction, and the public mind would, as for eighty years past, believe that it was in the course of ultimate extinction. The crisis would be passed and the institution might be let alone for a hundred years, if it should live so long, in the states where it exists, yet it would be going out of existence in the way best for both the black and the white races. [Great cheering.]

Douglas: I ask you [the audience], are you in favor of conferring upon the negro the rights and privileges of citizenship? ["No, no."] Do you desire to strike out of our state's constitution that clause which keeps slaves and free negroes out of the state, and allow the free negroes to flow in ["Never,"], and cover your prairies with black settlements? Do you desire to turn this beautiful State into a free negro colony ["No, no,"], in order that when Missouri abolishes slavery she can send one hundred thousand emancipated slaves into Illinois to become citizens and voters, on an equality with yourselves? ["Never," "no."] If you desire negro citizenship, if you desire to allow them to come into the state and settle with the white man, if you desire them to vote on an equality with yourselves, and to make them eligible to office, to serve on juries, and to adjudge your rights, then support Mr. Lincoln and the Black Republican party, who are in favor of the citizenship of the negro. ["Never, never."] For one, I am opposed to negro citizenship in any and every form. [Cheers.] I believe this Government was made on the white basis. ["Good."] I believe it was made by white men, for the benefit of white men and their posterity for ever, and I am in favor of confining citizenship to white men, men of European birth and descent, instead of conferring it upon negroes, Indians, and other inferior races. ["Good for you." "Douglas forever."]

Here Douglas makes what logicians and students of debate call a "slippery slope" or "parade of horribles" argument. Containing slavery, he implies, will lead to the demise of slavery, which will lead to African American citizenship and to African Americans leaving the South and populating the North. Why might such arguments have been effective before a Northern audience?

Now, I hold that Illinois had a right to abolish and prohibit slavery as she did, and I hold that Kentucky has the same right to continue and protect slavery that Illinois had to abolish it. I hold that New York had as much right to abolish slavery as Virginia has to continue it, and that each and every state of this Union is a sovereign power, with the right to do as it pleases upon this question of slavery, and upon all its domestic institutions.

Slavery is not the only question which comes up in this controversy. There is a far more important one to you, and that is: what shall be done with the free negro? We have said that they shall not vote, whilst Maine, on the other hand, has said that they shall vote. Maine is a sovereign state, and has the power to regulate the qualifications of voters within her limits. I would never consent to confer the right of voting and of citizenship upon a negro, but still I am not going to quarrel with Maine for differing from me in opinion. Let Maine take care of her own negroes and fix the qualifications of her own voters to suit herself, without interfering with Illinois, and Illinois will not interfere with Maine.

Our fathers intended that our institutions should differ. They knew that the North and the South, having different climates, productions and interests, required different institutions. This doctrine of Mr. Lincoln's of uniformity among the institutions of the different states, is a new doctrine, never dreamed of by Washington, Madison, or the framers of this government. Mr. Lincoln and the Republican party set themselves up as wiser than these men who made this government, which has flourished for seventy years under the principle of popular sovereignty, recognizing the right of each state to do as it pleased. Under that principle, we have grown from a nation of three or four millions to a nation of about thirty millions of people. We have crossed the Allegheny mountains and filled up the whole Northwest, turning the prairie into a garden, and building up churches and schools, thus spreading civilization and Christianity where before there was nothing but savage barbarism. Under that principle we have become, from a feeble nation, the most powerful on the face of the earth. If we only adhere to that principle, we can go forward increasing in territory, in power, in strength and in glory until the republic of America shall be the North Star that shall guide the friends of freedom throughout the civilized world. ["Long may you live," and great applause.]

I believe that this new doctrine preached by Mr. Lincoln and his party will dissolve the Union, if it succeeds. They are trying to array all the Northern states in one body against the South, to excite a sectional war between the free States and the slave states, in order that the one or the other may be driven to the wall.

＊

CHAPTER 2

Second Debate, Freeport, Illinois, August 27, 1858

At the end of the first debate in Ottawa, Lincoln had been surrounded by a pro-Republican crowd as he descended from the platform and had been carried on their shoulders around town as a brass band played "Hail, Columbia!" Lincoln was a little embarrassed by the hoopla (and Douglas would make him pay for it in Jonesboro), but overall he was quite pleased with his performance in Ottawa. "Douglas and I . . . crossed swords here yesterday," he wrote a friend. "The fire flew some, and I am glad to know I am yet alive." Living through a debate is hardly a high bar, but expectations for Lincoln had been so low that the fact that he had held his own was cause for celebration. Lyman Trumbull, Illinois's other sitting senator, wrote Lincoln that he had achieved nothing less than a "complete triumph over the little pettifogger," but Lincoln's handlers knew he could do even better. As Douglas had intended, Lincoln had spent most of the first debate on the defensive. In a single hour he had been forced to fend off charges that he was a radical, that he was conspiring to abolitionize both parties, that he advocated full racial equality, that he was seeking to dissolve the Union, and that he had betrayed his country in the Mexican War. Douglas, in short, had hit him with the kitchen sink, and Lincoln had done little more than defend and jab. "Your friends think that you ought not to treat him tenderly," an associate wrote Lincoln immediately after Ottawa. "He is try[ing] to intimidate you:—you have got to treat him severely and the sooner you commence the better."[5]

The second debate took place in Freeport, Illinois, a town in the extreme north of the state in a county bordering Wisconsin. Like La Salle, the county had gone for Fremont, although by an even wider margin, making it the most Republican-friendly site for any of the debates. The local organizers had secured an abandoned lot near the center of town and there erected a large square platform, sitting three feet off the ground, hewn from rough boards. The crowd itself was larger than it had been at Ottawa (perhaps 15,000), and it was also rowdier, although Douglas seemed to feed on their dark energy, lashing them relentlessly as Black Republicans. Here also Douglas was compelled to explain how, under Dred Scott, a territory could keep

*slavery out, an explanation that would come to be known as his Freeport Doctrine—
the notion that unfriendly local legislation can make slavery impossible to
police and therefore impossible to practice. This would cost him dearly among
Southern voters when he ran for president in 1860. For his part, Lincoln had
determined to take a more aggressive line, which he attempted to do by quickly
answering all of Douglas's questions from Ottawa and then propounding a few
of his own.*

Lincoln: *Ladies and gentlemen. In the course of [our] opening argument [in
Ottawa] Judge Douglas proposed to me seven distinct interrogatories. I now
propose that I will answer [them], upon condition that he will answer questions from me not exceeding the same number. I give him an opportunity to
respond. The Judge remains silent. I now say that I will answer his interrogatories, whether he answers mine or not; [applause] and that after I have done
so, I shall propound mine to him. [Applause.]*

*Question 1. "I desire to know whether Lincoln to-day stands, as he did in
1854, in favor of the unconditional repeal of the Fugitive Slave law?"*

*Answer. I do not now, nor ever did, stand in favor of the unconditional
repeal of the Fugitive Slave law. [Cries of "Good," "Good."]*

*Q. 2. "I desire him to answer whether he stands pledged to-day, as he did in
1854, against the admission of any more slave States into the Union, even if
the people want them?"*

*A. I do not now, or ever did, stand pledged against the admission of any
more slave states into the Union.*

*Q. 3. "I want to know whether he stands pledged against the admission of a
new state into the Union with such a Constitution as the people of that state
may see fit to make?"*

*A. I do not stand pledged against the admission of a new State into the
Union, with such a Constitution as the people of that state may see fit to
make. [Cries of "good," "good."]*

*Q. 4. "I want to know whether he stands to-day pledged to the abolition of
slavery in the District of Columbia?"*

*A. I do not stand to-day pledged to the abolition of slavery in the District of
Columbia.*

Q. 5. "I desire him to answer whether he stands pledged to the prohibition of the slave trade between the different states?"

A. I do not stand pledged to the prohibition of the slave trade between the different states.

Q. 6. "I desire to know whether he stands pledged to prohibit slavery in all the Territories of the United States, North as well as South of the Missouri Compromise line?"

A. I am impliedly, if not expressly, pledged to a belief in the right and duty of Congress to prohibit slavery in all the United States Territories.

Q. 7. "I desire him to answer whether he is opposed to the acquisition of any new territory unless slavery is first prohibited therein?"

A. I am not generally opposed to honest acquisition of territory; and, in any given case, I would or would not oppose such acquisition, accordingly as I might think such acquisition would or would not aggravate the slavery question among ourselves. [Cries of "good," "good."]

Now, my friends, it will be perceived upon an examination of these questions and answers, that so far I have only answered that I was not pledged to this, that, or the other. The Judge has not framed his interrogatories to ask me anything more than this, and I have answered in strict accordance with the interrogatories, and have answered truly that I am not pledged at all upon any of the points to which I have answered. But I am not disposed to hang upon the exact form of his interrogatory. I am rather disposed to take up at least some of these questions, and state what I really think upon them.

In regard to the abolition of slavery in the District of Columbia, I have my mind very distinctly made up. I should be exceedingly glad to see slavery abolished in the District of Columbia. [Cries of "good, good."] I believe that Congress possesses the constitutional power to abolish it. Yet as a member of Congress, I should not with my present views, be in favor of endeavoring to abolish slavery in the District of Columbia, unless it would be upon these conditions: First, that the abolition should be gradual; second, that it should be on a vote of the majority of qualified voters in the District; and third, that compensation should be made to unwilling owners. With these three conditions, I confess I would be exceedingly glad to see Congress abolish slavery in the District of Columbia and, in the language of Henry Clay, sweep from our capital that "foul blot" upon our nation. [Loud applause.]

In regard to the fifth interrogatory, I must say here that, as to the question of the abolition of the slave trade between the different states, I can truly answer, as I have, that I am pledged *to nothing about it. That question has never been prominently enough before me to induce me to investigate whether we really have the constitutional power to do it. I could investigate it if I had sufficient time and bring myself to a conclusion upon that subject, but I have not done so, and I say so frankly to you here, and to Judge Douglas. I must say, however, that if I should be of opinion that Congress does possess the constitutional power to abolish the slave trade among the different states, I should still not be in favor of the exercise of that power unless upon some conservative principle, as I conceive it, akin to what I have said in relation to the abolition of slavery in the District of Columbia.*

I now proceed to propound to the Judge the interrogatories, so far as I have framed them. I will bring forward a new installment when I get them ready. [Laughter.] I will bring them forward now, only reaching to number four.

The first one is: If the people of Kansas shall, by means entirely unobjectionable in all other respects, adopt a state constitution, and ask admission into the Union under it, before they have the requisite number of inhabitants— some ninety-three thousand—will you vote to admit them? [Applause.]

Douglas: *Ladies and Gentlemen: I am glad that at last I have brought Mr. Lincoln to the conclusion that he had better define his position on certain political questions to which I called his attention at Ottawa. He there showed no disposition, no inclination, to answer them. In a few moments I will proceed to review the answers which he has given to these interrogatories, but in order to relieve his anxiety I will first respond to those which he has presented to me.*

First, he desires to know if the people of Kansas shall form a constitution by means entirely proper and unobjectionable and ask admission into the Union as a state, before they have the requisite population for a member of Congress, whether I will vote for that admission. It is my opinion, that as she has population enough to constitute a slave state, she has people enough for a free state. [Cheers.] I will not make Kansas an exceptional case to the other states of the Union. ["Sound," and "hear, hear."]

Lincoln: *Question 2. Can the people of a United States territory, in any lawful way, against the wish of any citizen of the United States, exclude slavery from its limits prior to the formation of a state constitution? [Applause, cheers.]*

Douglas: *I answer emphatically, as Mr. Lincoln has heard me answer a hundred times from every stump in Illinois, that in my opinion the people of a territory can, by lawful means, exclude slavery from their limits prior to the formation of a state constitution. Mr. Lincoln knew that I had answered that question over and over again. He heard me argue the Nebraska bill on that principle all over the State in 1854, in 1855, and in 1856, and he has no excuse for pretending to be in doubt as to my position on that question. It matters*

*not what way the Supreme Court may hereafter decide as to the abstract
question whether slavery may or may not go into a territory under the Constitution. The people have the lawful means to introduce it or exclude it as they
please, for the reason that slavery cannot exist a day or an hour anywhere,
unless it is supported by local police regulations. ["Right, right."] Those police
regulations can only be established by the local legislature, and if the people
are opposed to slavery, they will elect representatives to that body who will, by
unfriendly legislation, effectually prevent the introduction of it into their midst.
If, on the contrary, they are for it, their legislation will favor its extension.
Hence, no matter what the decision of the Supreme Court may be on that
abstract question, still the right of the people to make a slave territory or
a free territory is perfect and complete under the Nebraska bill. I hope
Mr. Lincoln deems my answer satisfactory on that point.*

Obviously, the Supreme Court's decision in *Dred Scott* was a catastrophe for Republicans, whose main platform—restricting slavery's spread—presumed the federal government's right to determine the status, free or slave, of a territory. In less
obvious ways, the *Scott* decision was awkward for Douglas because its end logic
suggested that slaves were just another species of property and were legally protected everywhere, including "free" states. This was a potential catastrophe for
Douglas's doctrine of "popular sovereignty," which held that territories could
decide for themselves whether they wanted slavery. Douglas's "work around,"
which he outlines here, came to be called the "Freeport Doctrine." What do you
think of his argument? How, in a sense, had the Supreme Court created a difficult
situation for *both* Lincoln and Douglas? Which man had the better work around
for the *Scott* decision?

*Lincoln: Question 3. If the Supreme Court of the United States shall decide
that states can not exclude slavery from their limits, are you in favor of acqui-
escing in, adopting, and following such decision as a rule of political action?
[Loud applause.]*

   *Douglas: I am amazed that Lincoln should ask such a question. ["A school
boy knows better."] Yes, a school boy does know better. He might as well ask
me, suppose Mr. Lincoln should steal a horse, would I sanction it. [Laughter.]
And it would be as genteel in me to ask him, in the event he stole a horse,
what ought to be done with him. He casts an imputation upon the Supreme
Court of the United States by supposing that they would violate the Constitution of the United States. I tell him that such a thing is not possible. [Cheers.]
It would be an act of moral treason that no man on the bench could ever*

descend to. Mr. Lincoln himself would never, in his partisan feelings, so far
forget what was right as to be guilty of such an act. ["Good, good."]

Lincoln: Question 4. Are you in favor of acquiring additional territory, in
disregard of how such acquisition may affect the nation on the slavery question? [Cries of "good," "good."]

Douglas: I answer that whenever it becomes necessary, in our growth and
progress, to acquire more territory, that I am in favor of it, without reference
to the question of slavery. And when we have acquired it, I will leave the
people free to do as they please, either to make it slave or free territory, as they
prefer. ["That's bold."] You cannot limit this great republic by mere boundary
lines, saying, "thus far shalt thou go, and no further." Any one of you gentlemen might as well say to a son twelve years old that he is big enough, and
must not grow any larger, and in order to prevent his growth put a hoop
around him to keep him to his present size. What would be the result? Either
the hoop must burst and be rent asunder, or the child must die. [Laughter.] So
it would be with this great nation. With our natural increase, growing with
rapidity unknown in any other part of the globe, with the tide of emigration
that is fleeing from despotism in the old world to seek refuge in our own, there
is a constant torrent pouring into this country that requires more land, more
territory upon which to settle. And just as fast as our interests and our destiny
require additional territory in the North, in the South, or on the islands of the
ocean, I am for it, and when we acquire it will leave the people, according to
the Nebraska bill, free to do as they please on the subject of slavery and every
other question. ["Good, good," and "hurrah for Douglas."]

I trust now that Mr. Lincoln will deem himself answered on his four points.
He racked his brain so much in devising these four questions that he exhausted
himself, and had not strength enough to invent the others. [Laughter.] As soon
as he is able to hold a council with his advisers—Lovejoy, Farnsworth, and
Fred Douglass—he will frame and propound others. ["Good, good," and re-
newed laughter.] You Black Republicans who say "good," I have no doubt
think that they are all good men. ["White, white."] I have reason to recollect
that some people in this country think that Fred Douglass is a very good man.
The last time I came here to make a speech, while talking from the stand to
you people of Freeport, as I am doing today, I saw a carriage, and a magnifi-
cent one it was, drive up and take a position on the outside of the crowd, a
beautiful young lady was sitting on the box seat, whilst Fred Douglass and her
mother reclined inside, and the owner of the carriage acted as driver. [Laugh-
ter, cheers, cries of "right," "what have you to say against it?"] I saw this in
your own town. ["What of it?"] All I have to say of it is this—that if you, Black
Republicans think that the negro ought to be on a social equality with your
wives and daughters and ride in a carriage with your wife, whilst you drive the
team, you have perfect right to do so. I am told that one of Fred Douglass'
kinsmen, another rich black negro, is now traveling in this part of the State

making speeches for his friend Lincoln as the champion of black men. ["White men, white men," and "what have you to say against it?" "That's right."] *All I have to say on that subject is, that those of you who believe that the nigger is your equal and ought to be on an equality with you socially, politically, and legally, have a right to entertain those opinions, and of course will vote for Mr. Lincoln.* ["Down with the negro," "no, no," &c.]

I [want to] now read the resolutions adopted at the Rockford [Republican] Convention on the 30th of August, 1854:

Resolved, That we accept this issue forced upon us by the slave power, and, in defense of freedom, will co-operate and be known as Republicans, pledged to the accomplishment of the following purposes [including] to repeal and entirely abrogate the fugitive slave law.

In the adoption of that platform, you [speaking to Republicans on stage and in the audience] not only declared that you would resist the admission of any more slave states, and work for the repeal of the Fugitive Slave law, but you pledged yourselves not to vote for any man for State or Federal offices who was not committed to these principles. You were thus committed. Similar resolutions to those were adopted in your county convention here, and now what do you think of Mr. Lincoln, your candidate for the U. S. Senate, who is attempting to dodge the responsibility of this platform. When I get into the next district, I will show that the same platform was adopted there, and so on through the State, until I nail the responsibility of it upon the back of the Black Republican party throughout the state. ["White, white," "three cheers for Douglas."]

[A voice—"Couldn't you modify and call it brown?" Laughter.]

Douglas: Not a bit. I thought that you were becoming a little brown when your members in Congress voted for the Crittenden–Montgomery bill, but since you have backed out from that position and gone back to abolitionism, you are black and not brown. [Shouts of laughter.]

It has been published to the world and satisfactorily proven that there was, at the time the alliance was made between Trumbull and Lincoln to abolitionize the two parties, an agreement that Lincoln should take Shields's place in the United States Senate, and Trumbull should have mine so soon as they could conveniently get rid of me. [Laughter.] *When Lincoln was beaten for Shields's place, he felt very sore and restive. His friends grumbled, and some of them came out and charged that the most infamous treachery had been practiced against him; that the bargain was that Lincoln was to have had Shields's place, and Trumbull was to have waited for mine, but that Trumbull having the control of a few abolitionized Democrats, he prevented them from voting for Lincoln, thus keeping him within a few votes of an election until he succeeded in forcing the party to drop him and elect Trumbull. Well, Trumbull having cheated Lincoln, his friends made a fuss, and in order to keep them and Lincoln quiet, the party were obliged to come forward, in advance, at the*

*last state election, and make a pledge that they would go for Lincoln and
nobody else. Lincoln could not be silenced in any other way.*

*Now, there are a great many Black Republicans of you who do not know
this thing was done. ["White, white," and great clamor.] I wish to remind you
that while Mr. Lincoln was speaking there was not a Democrat vulgar and
blackguard enough to interrupt him. But I know that the shoe is pinching you.
I am clinching Lincoln now, and you are scared to death for the result.
[Cheers.] I have seen this thing before. I have seen men make appointments
for joint discussions, and the moment their man has been heard, try to interrupt and prevent a fair hearing of the other side. I have seen your mobs before,
and defy your wrath. [Tremendous applause.]*

What do you think of Douglas's persistence in calling his political adversaries the
"Black" Republicans, even in the face of stiff resistance from the crowd? Do you
think he is feeding on the dark energy of the throng, or do you think he let his
emotions get the better of him? Could a politician today say, "I defy your wrath!"?

*There is no dodging the question. I want Lincoln's answer. He says he was not
pledged to repeal the Fugitive Slave Law, that he does not quite like to do it.
He will not introduce a law to repeal it, but thinks there ought to be some law.
He does not tell what it ought to be. Upon the whole, he is altogether undecided, and don't know what to think or do. That is the substance of his answer
upon the repeal of the Fugitive Slave Law. I put the question to him distinctly,
whether he endorsed that part of the Black Republican platform which calls
for the entire abrogation and repeal of the Fugitive Slave Law. He answers no,
that he does not endorse that, but he does not tell what he is for, or what he
will vote for. His answer is, in fact, no answer at all. Why cannot he speak out
and say what he is for and what he will do? Why cannot your Black Republican candidates talk out as plain as that when they are questioned?*

*Lincoln: My friends: The first thing I have to say to you is a word in regard
to Judge Douglas's declaration about the "vulgarity and blackguardism" in the
audience—that no such thing, as he says, was shown by any Democrat while I
was speaking. Now, I only wish, by way of reply on this subject, to say that
while I was speaking, I used no "vulgarity or blackguardism" toward any Democrat. [Great laughter and applause.]*

*Now, my friends, I come to all this long portion of the Judge's speech—per-
haps half of it—which he has devoted to the various resolutions and platforms
that have been adopted in the different counties in the different congressional*

districts, and in the Illinois legislature—which he supposes are at variance with the positions I have assumed before you today. It is true that many of these resolutions are at variance with the positions I have here assumed. All I have to ask is that we talk reasonably and rationally about it. The plain truth is this: At the introduction of the Nebraska policy, we believed there was a new era being introduced in the history of the republic, which tended to the spread and perpetuation of slavery. But in our opposition to that measure we did not agree with one another in every thing. The people in the north end of the state were for stronger measures of opposition than we of the central and southern portions of the state, but we were all opposed to the Nebraska doctrine. We had that one feeling and that one sentiment in common. You at the north end met in your conventions and passed your resolutions. We in the middle of the state and further south did not hold such conventions and pass the same reso-lutions, although we had in general a common view and a common senti-ment. So that these meetings which the Judge has alluded to, and the [Rockford] resolutions he has read from, were local, and did not spread over the whole state. We at last met together in 1856, from all parts of the state, and we agreed upon a common platform. You, who held more extreme no-tions, either yielded those notions, or if not wholly yielding them, agreed to yield them practically, for the sake of embodying the opposition to the mea-sures which the opposite party were pushing forward at that time. We met you then, and if there was any thing yielded, it was for practical purposes. We agreed then upon a platform for the party throughout the entire State of Illi-nois, and now we are all bound as a party, to that platform. And I say here to you, if any one expects of me—in the case of my election—that I will do any thing not signified by our Republican platform and my answers here today, I tell you very frankly that person will be deceived. I do not ask for the vote of any one who supposes that I have secret purposes or pledges that I dare not speak out. Cannot the Judge be satisfied? If he fears, in the unfortunate case of my election [laughter], that my going to Washington will enable me to advocate sentiments contrary to those which I expressed when you voted for and elected me, I assure him that his fears are wholly needless and groundless. Is the Judge really afraid of any such thing? [Laughter.] I'll tell you what he is afraid of. He is afraid we'll all pull together. *[Applause, and cries of "We will, we will."] This is what alarms him more than anything else. [Laughter.] For my part, I do hope that all of us, entertaining a common sentiment in opposition to what appears to us a design to nationalize and perpetuate slav-ery, will waive minor differences on questions which either belong to the dead past or the distant future, and all pull together in this struggle. What are your sentiments? ["We will, we will," and loud cheers.] If it be true, that on the ground which I occupy—ground which I occupy as frankly and boldly as Judge Douglas does his—my views, though partly coinciding with yours, are not as perfectly in accordance with your feelings as his are, I do say to you in all candor, go for him and not for me. I hope to deal in all things fairly with Judge Douglas, and with the people of the State, in this contest. And if I should never be elected to any office, I trust I may go down with no stain of falsehood upon my reputation, notwithstanding the hard opinions Judge Douglas chooses to entertain of me. [Laughter.]*

CHAPTER 3

Third Debate, Jonesboro, Illinois, September 15, 1858

After the second debate in Freeport, Illinois, Senator Lyman Trumbull correctly predicted that, when properly made to answer for it, Douglas's Freeport Doctrine "would effectually use him up with the South & set the whole proslavery Democracy against him." But if Douglas had sewn the seeds of his national unraveling at Freeport, he did not seem to know it, nor particularly did Lincoln. After two debates on largely Republican terrain, the men now turned to southern Illinois, a region nicknamed "Little Egypt" after its commercial center in the town of Cairo, the southernmost city in the free states. The area was a Democratic stronghold, friendly to Douglas, but the actual debate took place in Jonesboro, a small byway of a town with a population of just 1,000, the seat of Union County, one of the poorest and least educated in the state. Turnout in Jonesboro was predictably poor, probably just 1,500, roughly one-tenth the size of the crowd that had assembled to hear the candidates in Freeport. Lincoln had little chance of winning these voters over and his performance was not particularly inspired or inspiring. Douglas too began by rehashing earlier speeches in what one witness called a "school boy monotone." (Perhaps with no crowd to feed upon, Douglas took a while to warm up.) But if the Jonesboro debate generated little light, it generated a good deal of heat as both men mixed it up in attacks that were less political than they were personal.[16]

Douglas: *Ladies and gentlemen: I appear before you today in pursuance of a previous notice, and have made arrangements with Mr. Lincoln to divide time and discuss with him the leading political topics that now agitate the country.*

In 1854, certain restless, ambitious, and disappointed politicians throughout the land took advantage of the temporary excitement created by the Nebraska bill to try and dissolve the old Whig party and the old Democratic party, to abolitionize their members, and lead them, bound hand and foot, captives into the abolition camp. I am doing no more than justice to the truth of history when I say that in this state Abraham Lincoln, on behalf of the Whigs, and Lyman Trumbull, on behalf of the Democrats, were the leaders who undertook to perform this grand scheme of abolitionizing the two parties to which they belonged.

In the extreme northern counties they brought out men to canvass the state whose complexion suited their political creed, and hence Fred Douglass, the negro, was to be found there, following General Cass, and attempting to speak on behalf of Lincoln, Trumbull and abolitionism, against that illustrious senator. [Laughter.] Why, they brought Fred Douglass to Freeport, when I was addressing a meeting there, in a carriage driven by the white owner, the negro sitting inside with the white lady and her daughter. ["Shame."] When I got through canvassing the northern counties that year and progressed as far south as Springfield, I was met and opposed in discussion by Lincoln, Lovejoy, Trumbull, and Sidney Breese, who were on one side. [Laughter.] Father Giddings, the high priest of abolitionism, had just been there, and Chase came about the time I left. ["Why didn't you shoot him?"] I did take a running shot at them, but as I was single-handed against the white, black and mixed drove, I had to use a shotgun and fire into the crowd instead of taking them off singly with a rifle. [Great laughter and cheers.]

Does it surprise you that Douglas would make a joke about firing into a (fictitious) crowd? How is he hoping to connect with voters in making this joke?

Now these men, four years ago, were engaged in a conspiracy to break down the Democracy. Today they are again acting together for the same purpose!

Lincoln: Now, fellow citizens, in regard to this matter about a contract that was made between Judge Trumbull and myself, and all that long portion of Judge Douglas's speech on this subject, I wish simply to say what I have said to him before, that he cannot know whether it is true or not, and I do know that there is not a word of truth in it. [Applause.] And I have told him so before. [Continued applause, "That's right." "Hit him again."] I don't want any harsh language indulged in, but I do not know how to deal with this persistent insisting on a story that I know to be utterly without truth. It used to be a fashion amongst men that when a charge was made, some sort of proof was brought forward to establish it, and if no proof was found to exist, the charge was dropped. I don't know how to meet this kind of an argument. I don't want to have a fight with Judge Douglas, and I have no way of making an argument up into the consistency of a corn cob and stopping his mouth with it. [Laughter and applause.] All I can do is, good-humoredly to say that, from the beginning to the end of all that story about a bargain between Judge Trumbull and myself, there is not a word of truth in it. [Applause.]

Douglas: I wish to invite your attention to the chief points at issue between Mr. Lincoln and myself in this discussion. Mr. Lincoln, knowing that he was to be the candidate of his party on account of the arrangement of which I have already spoken, knowing that he was to receive the nomination of the convention for the United States Senate, had his speech, accepting that nomination, all written and committed to memory, a portion of which I will read, in order that I may state his political principles fairly, by repeating them in his own language:

"We are now far into the fifth year since a policy was instituted for the avowed object, and with the confident promise of putting an end to slavery agitation; under the operation of that policy, that agitation has not only not ceased, but has constantly augmented. I believe it will not cease until a crisis shall have been reached and passed. 'A house divided against itself cannot stand.' I believe this Government cannot endure permanently half slave and half free. I do not expect the Union to be dissolved—I do not expect the house to fall—but I do expect it will cease to be divided. It will become all one thing or all the other. Either the opponents of slavery will arrest the spread of it, and place it where the public mind shall rest in the belief that it is in the course of ultimate extinction, or its advocates will push it forward until it shall become alike lawful in all the states—North as well as South."

There you have Mr. Lincoln's first and main proposition, upon which he bases his claims, stated in his own language. He tells you that this republic cannot endure permanently divided into slave and free States, as our fathers made it. He says that they must all become free or all become slave, that they must all be one thing or all be the other, or this government cannot last. Mr. Lincoln likens that bond of the federal Constitution joining free and slave states together to a house divided against itself and says that it is contrary to the law of God and cannot stand. Where did he learn, and by what authority does he proclaim, that this Government is contrary to the law of God and cannot stand? It has stood thus divided into free and slave states from its organization up to this day. During that period we have increased from four millions to thirty millions of people. We have extended our territory from the Mississippi to the Pacific Ocean. We have acquired the Floridas and Texas and other territory sufficient to double our geographical extent. We have increased in population, in wealth, and in naval and military power beyond any example on earth. We have risen from a weak and feeble power to become the terror and admiration of the civilized world. And all this has been done under a Constitution which Mr. Lincoln, in substance, says is in violation of the law of God.

Lincoln: Ladies and gentlemen: In so far as [Judge Douglas] has insisted that all the states have the right to do exactly as they please about all their domestic relations, including that of slavery, I agree entirely with him. He *places me wrong in spite of all I can tell him, though I repeat it again and again, insisting that I have no difference with him upon this subject. I have made a great many speeches, some of which have been printed, and it will be utterly impossible for him to find any thing that I have ever put in print contrary to what I now say upon this subject. I hold myself under constitutional obligations to allow the people in all the States, without interference, direct or indirect, to do exactly as they please, and I deny that I have any inclination to interfere with them, even if there were no such constitutional obligation.*

Judge Douglas says, "Why can't this Union endure permanently, half slave and half free?" I have said that I supposed it could not, and I will try, before this new audience, to give briefly some of the reasons for entertaining that opinion. Another form of his question is, "Why can't we let it stand as our fathers placed it?" That is the exact difficulty between us. I say, in the way our fathers originally left the slavery question, the institution was in the course of ultimate extinction, and the public mind rested in the belief that it was in the course of ultimate extinction. I say when this Government was first established, it was the policy of its founders to prohibit the spread of slavery into the new territories of the United States, where it had not existed. But Judge Douglas and his friends have broken up that policy and placed it upon a new basis by which it is to become national and perpetual. All I have asked or desired anywhere is that it should be placed back again upon the basis that the fathers of our government originally placed it upon. I have no doubt that it would become extinct, for all time to come, if we but re-adopted the policy of the fathers by restricting it to the limits it has already covered, restricting it from the new territories.

Brooks, the man who assaulted Senator Sumner on the floor of the Senate, and who was complimented with dinners, and silver pitchers, and gold-headed canes and a good many other things for that feat, in one of his speeches declared that when this Government was originally established, nobody expected that the institution of slavery would last until this day. That was but the opinion of one man, but it was such an opinion as we can never get from Judge Douglas or anybody in favor of slavery in the North at all. You can sometimes get it from a Southern man. He said at the same time that the framers of our Government did not have the knowledge that experience has taught us, that experience and the invention of the cotton-gin have taught us that the perpetuation of slavery is a necessity. He insisted, therefore, upon its being changed from the basis upon which the fathers of the government left it to the basis of its perpetuation and nationalization. I insist that this is the difference between Judge Douglas and myself—that Judge Douglas is helping that change along.

Lincoln makes the case that the Founders put slavery on the road to ultimate extinction but that, instead of dying, the institution was expanding. What does he think happened? What does he mean when he says that Douglas is "helping that change along"?

Douglas: *[But] the Dred Scott decision covers [this] whole question, and declares that each state has the right to settle this question of [negro] suffrage for itself, and all questions as to the relations between the white man and the negro. Judge Taney expressly lays down the doctrine. I receive it as law, and I say that while those States are adopting regulations on that subject, disgusting and abhorrent, according to my views, I will not make war on them if they will mind their own business and let us alone.* ["Bravo," and cheers.]

We must bear in mind that we are yet a young nation growing with a rapidity unequaled in the history of the world, that our natural increase is great, and that the emigration from the old world is increasing, requiring us to expand and acquire new territory from time to time, in order to give our people land to live upon. If we live upon the principle of state rights and state sovereignty, each state regulating its own affairs and minding its own business, we can go on and extend indefinitely, just as fast and as far as we need the territory. The time may come, indeed has now come, when our interests would be advanced by the acquisition of the island of Cuba. [Terrific applause.] *When we get Cuba we must take it as we find it, leaving the people to decide the question of slavery for themselves, without interference on the part of the federal government, or of any state of this Union.*

The great mission of the Democracy is to unite the fraternal feeling of the whole country, restore peace and quiet by teaching each state to mind its own business, and regulate its own domestic affairs, and all to unite in carrying out the Constitution as our fathers made it, and thus to preserve the Union and render it perpetual in all time to come. Why should we not act as our fathers who made the government? There was no sectional strife in Washington's army. They were all brethren of a common confederacy. They fought under a common flag that they might bestow upon their posterity a common destiny, and to this end they poured out their blood in common streams, and shared, in some instances a common grave. [Three hearty cheers for Douglas.]

Lincoln: *In the first place, the Supreme Court of the United States has decided that any congressional prohibition of slavery in the territories is unconstitutional. Hence they reach the conclusion that the Constitution of the United States expressly recognizes property in slaves, and prohibits any person from being deprived of property without due process of law [on any] side of a line. That I understand to be the decision of the Supreme Court. I understand also that Judge Douglas adheres most firmly to that decision; and the difficulty is: How is it possible for any power to exclude slavery from [any] territory unless in violation of that decision? That is the difficulty.*

I hold that [Judge Douglas's] proposition [propounded at Freeport] that slavery cannot enter a new country without police regulations is historically false. It is not true at all. I hold that the history of this country shows that the institution of slavery was originally planted upon this continent without *these "police regulations" which the Judge now thinks necessary for the actual establishment of it.*

I will ask you, my friends, if you were elected members of the legislature, what would be the first thing you would have to do before entering upon your duties? Swear to support the Constitution of the United States. *Suppose you believe, as Judge Douglas does, that the Constitution of the United States guaranties to your neighbor the right to hold slaves [anywhere], that they are his property. How can you clear your oaths unless you give him such legislation as is necessary to enable him to enjoy that property? How could you, having sworn to support the Constitution and believing it guarantied the right to hold slaves in the territories, assist in legislation* intended to defeat that right? *That would be violating your own view of the Constitution.*

Now, my fellow-citizens, I will detain you only a little while longer. I find a report of a speech made by Judge Douglas at Joliet, since we last met at Freeport, published, I believe, in the Missouri Republican *on the ninth of this month, in which Judge Douglas says:*

"You know at Ottawa, I read this platform, and asked him if he concurred in each and all of the principles set forth in it. He would not answer these questions. At last I said frankly, I want you to answer them, because when I get you up where the color of your principles are a little darker than in Egypt, I intend to trot you down to Jonesboro. The very notice that I was going to take him down to Egypt made him tremble in the knees, so that he had to be carried from the platform. He laid up seven days, and in the meantime held a consultation with his political physicians. They had Lovejoy and Farnsworth and all the leaders of the Abolition party. They consulted it all over, and at last Lincoln came to the conclusion that he would answer, so he came up to Freeport last Friday."

Now that statement altogether furnishes a subject for philosophical contemplation. [Laughter.] *I have been treating it in that way, and I have really come to the conclusion that I can explain it in no other way than by believing the Judge is crazy.* [Laughter.] *If he was in his right mind, I cannot conceive how he would have risked disgusting the four or five thousand of his own friends who stood there, and knew, as to my having been carried from the platform, that there was not a word of truth in it.*

Douglas: *Didn't they carry you off?*

Lincoln: *There! That question illustrates the character of this man Douglas exactly. He smiles now and says, "Didn't they carry you off?" But he said then, "He had to be carried off." And he said it to convince the country that he had so completely broken me down by his speech that I had to be carried away. Now he seeks to dodge it, and asks, "Didn't they carry you off?" Yes, they did. But, Judge Douglas, why didn't you tell the truth?* [Laughter, cheers.] *I would like to know why you didn't tell the truth about it.*

Douglas: *I did.*

Lincoln: *And then again, "He laid up seven days." He puts this in print for the people of the country to read as a serious document. I think if he had been in his sober senses he would not have risked that barefacedness in the presence of thousands of his own friends, who knew that I made speeches within six of the seven days at Henry, Marshall County; Augusta, Hancock County; and Macomb, McDonough County, including all the necessary travel to meet him again at Freeport at the end of the six days. Now, I say, there is no charitable way to look at that statement, except to conclude that he is actually crazy.* [Laughter.]

There is another thing in that statement that alarmed me very greatly as he states it, that he was going to "trot me down to Egypt." Thereby he would have you to infer that I would not come to Egypt unless he forced me, that I could not be got here, unless he, giant-like, had hauled me down here. [Laughter.] *More than all this, Judge Douglas, when he made that statement, must have been crazy, and wholly out of his sober senses, or else he would have known that when he got me down here, that promise, that windy promise, of his powers to annihilate me, wouldn't amount to anything. Did the Judge talk of trotting me down to Egypt to scare me to death? Why, I know this people better than he does. I was raised just a little east of here. I am a part of this people. But the Judge was raised further north, and perhaps he has some horrid idea of what this people might be induced to do. The Judge has set about seriously trying to make the impression that when we meet at different places I am literally in his clutches, that I am a poor, helpless, decrepit mouse, and that I can do nothing at all. I don't want to quarrel with him, to call him a liar, but when I come square up to him I don't know what else to call him, if I must tell the truth out.* [Cheers and laughter.]

I want to be at peace, and reserve all my fighting powers for necessary occasions. My time, now, is very nearly out, and I give up the trifle that is left to the Judge, to let him set my knees trembling again, if he can.

Douglas: *My friends, while I am very grateful to you for the enthusiasm which you show for me, I will say in all candor, that your quietness will be much more agreeable than your applause, in as much as you deprive me of some part of my time whenever you cheer.* ["All right," "go ahead," "we won't interrupt," &c.]

I will commence where Mr. Lincoln left off, and make a remark upon this serious complaint of his about my speech at Joliet. I did say there in a playful manner that when I put these questions to Mr. Lincoln at Ottawa, he failed to answer, and that he trembled and had to be carried off the stand, and required seven days to get up his reply. [Laughter.] *That he did not walk off from*

*that stand he will not deny. That when the crowd went away from the stand
with me, a few persons carried him home on their shoulders and laid him
down, he will admit. [Shouts of laughter.] I wish to say to you that whenever I
degrade my friends and myself by allowing them to carry me on their backs
along through the public streets when I am able to walk, I am willing to be
deemed crazy. ["All right, Douglas," laughter and applause.]*

Earlier in the nineteenth century, duels were relatively common, even in the North.
According to the code duello, assaults on a man's *political* character were supposed
to be borne; a true gentleman was supposed to weather even severe criticism and
stand stoically by his principles. If the assault against his political character became
embittered and exaggerated, the man might seek redress in court, and many
famous gentleman-politicians carried on an elaborate array of libel cases against
their detractors. In the case of attacks on a man's *personal* character, however, he
was expected to seek satisfaction on the field of honor. This system persisted much
longer in the South, but do you see vestiges of this "honor culture" in the preceding
exchange between Lincoln and Douglas? Do you suppose Lincoln really is angry
about Douglas's portrait of him as a "poor, helpless, decrepit mouse"? Or is he just
trying to score some political points in an age when politics was (sometimes literally) combative? Both men clearly believe it was an indignity to be carried, even by
your partisans. What does this suggest about masculinity in this period? Do you
see other examples where the men's masculinity or sense of honor is in play?

*Mr. Lincoln attempts to cover up and get over his abolitionism by telling you
that he was raised a little east of you [laughter], beyond the Wabash in Indiana, and he thinks that makes a mighty sound and good man of him on all
these questions. I do not know that the place where a man is born or raised
has much to do with his political principles. The worst abolitionists I have ever
known in Illinois have been men who have sold their slaves in Alabama and
Kentucky, and have come here and turned abolitionists whilst spending the
money got for the negroes they sold ["That's so," and laughter]. And I do not
know that an abolitionist from Indiana or Kentucky ought to have any more
credit because he was born and raised among slaveholders. ["Not a bit," "not
as much," &c.]*

*True, I was not born out west here. I was born away down in Yankee land
["Good"]. I was born in a valley in Vermont ["All right"] with the high mountains around me. I love the old green mountains and valleys of Vermont,
where I was born, and where I played in my childhood. I went up to visit them*

some seven or eight years ago, for the first time for twenty odd years. When I got there they treated me very kindly. They invited me to the commencement of their college, placed me on the seats with their distinguished guests, and conferred upon me the degree of L.L.D. in Latin, the same as they did old Hickory, at Cambridge, many years ago. And I give you my word and honor I understood just as much of the Latin as he did. [Laughter.] When they got through conferring the honorary degree, they called upon me for a speech, and I got up with my heart full and swelling with gratitude for their kindness, and I said to them, "My friends, Vermont is the most glorious spot on the face of this globe for a man to be born in, provided he emigrates when he is very young." [Uproarious shouts of laughter.]

I emigrated when I was very young. I came out here when I was a boy, and I found my mind liberalized and my opinions enlarged when I got on these broad prairies, with only the heavens to bound my vision, instead of having them circumscribed by the little narrow ridges that surrounded the valley where I was born. But, I discard all flings of the land where a man was born. I wish to be judged by my principles, by those great public measures and Constitutional principles upon which the peace, the happiness, and the perpetuity of this republic now rest.

We come right back, therefore, to the practical question, if the people of a territory want slavery they will have it, and if they do not want it, you cannot force it on them. And this is the practical question, the great principle, upon which our institutions rest. ["That's the doctrine."] I am willing to take the decision of the Supreme Court as it was pronounced by that august tribunal without stopping to inquire whether I would have decided that way or not. I have had many a decision made against me on questions of law which I did not like, but I was bound by them just as much as if I had had a hand in making them, and approved them. Did you ever see a lawyer who lost his case and liked the decision or a client who did not think the decision unjust? They always think the decision unjust when it is given against them. In a government of laws, like ours, we must sustain the Constitutions as our fathers made it, and maintain the rights of the States as they are guarantied under the Constitution; sustain the constitutional authorities as they exist, and then we will have peace and harmony between the different States and sections of this glorious Union. [Prolonged cheering.]

*

CHAPTER 4

Fourth Debate, Charleston, Illinois, September 18, 1858

After the Jonesboro debate, both campaigns swung into the center of the state, the so-called "Whig belt," where Republicans and Democrats stood on roughly equal footing and where, for all practical purposes, the Senatorial election would be won or lost. The site for the fourth debate, Charleston, Illinois, was located about ninety miles due east of Springfield, in Coles County, well known to Lincoln as the home of his stepmother. The area was vaguely antislavery but, having been settled predominately by ex-slaveholders, was also deeply white supremacist. In Ottawa and Freeport, in the north of the state, Douglas had largely leashed his race-baiting; he had been a little more outspoken in Jonesboro, but in Little Egypt racist appeals were almost assumed and unnecessary to carry the contest. Douglas came to Charleston, however, determined to put the racial questions at the front of the campaign. In a speech in Centralia the night before the debate, he delivered a crackling stem-winder, dilating with particular severity "on the unfortunate odor of the black man" and asking his audience if they wished "to eat with, ride with, go to church with, travel with, and in other ways bring Congo odor into their nostrils." In the first three debates, Lincoln had been careful always to insist that although African Americans were naturally equal, they were not (at least at present) socially equal. This distinction was too fine for many of his handlers and constituents. "They insist on identifying us with the Abolitionists in all their fanaticism," wrote one advisor, "& this point should be largely dwelt on by yourself [for] there is little sympathy [here] for the nigger." At Charleston, a pro-Douglas faction arranged a huge sign so that Lincoln would have to deliver his speech under a broad banner sarcastically proclaiming "Negro Equality." As a lawyer, and as a politician, Lincoln typically led with the things he didn't want to talk about, in the hope that he could get them out of the way. At Charleston, Lincoln said things that all lovers of Lincoln wish he had never said and most think he didn't fully believe. There is no denying he said them, however, and if he thought it would placate Douglas he was deeply mistaken.[17]

If Lincoln lost ground, with the voters and with history, for the weaselly way he dealt with race at Charleston, he scored far more political points on a subject now lost to time—the so-called "Toombs' bill." The 1857 Toombs Bill had been an attempt by Georgia senator Robert Toombs to end the violence in Kansas between the pro-slavery and antislavery factions vying for control of the state. Toombs suggested terminating Kansas's territorial status, conducting a federally supervised census to determine who the legal voters were in Kansas, and holding a federally supervised election to a convention charged with drawing up a new state constitution that would say whatever it wanted about slavery, and then that constitution would be referred back to the voters for a popular referendum. This was, in essence, Douglas's popular sovereignty in action. But when it went into Douglas's Committee on Territories it came out again without the clause requiring the popular referendum. To Illinois senator Lyman Trumbull this showed Douglas's true colors—he was not for popular sovereignty; he was for placating the South and broadening his political base. Lincoln had been repeatedly urged to make the most of this "conspiracy" and in Charleston, he would.

Lincoln: *Ladies and gentlemen: It will be very difficult for an audience so large as this to hear distinctly what a speaker says, and consequently it is important that as profound silence be preserved as possible.*

While I was at the hotel today, an elderly gentleman called upon me to know whether I was really in favor of producing a perfect equality between the negroes and white people. [Great laughter.] While I had not proposed to myself on this occasion to say much on that subject, yet as the question was asked me, I thought I would occupy perhaps five minutes in saying something in regard to it. I will say then that I am not, nor ever have been, in favor of bringing about in any way the social and political equality of the white and black races [applause]; that I am not nor ever have been in favor of making voters or jurors of negroes, nor of qualifying them to hold office, nor to intermarry with white people. And I will say in addition to this that there is a physical difference between the white and black races which I believe will forever forbid the two races living together on terms of social and political equality. And in as much as they cannot so live, while they do remain together there must be the position of superior and inferior, and I as much as any other man am in favor of having the superior position assigned to the white race. I say upon this occasion I do not perceive that because the white man is to have the superior position the negro should be denied everything. I do not understand that because I do not want a negro woman for a slave I must necessarily want her for a wife. [Cheers and laughter.] My understanding is that I can just let her alone. I am now in my fiftieth year, and I certainly never have had a black woman for either a slave or a wife. So it seems to me quite possible for us to get along without making either slaves or wives of negroes.

I will add to this that I have never seen, to my knowledge, a man, woman or child who was in favor of producing a perfect equality, social and political, between negroes and white men. I recollect of but one distinguished instance that I ever heard of so frequently as to be entirely satisfied of its correctness, and that is the case of Judge Douglas's old friend Col. Richard M. Johnson. [Laughter, cheers.] *I will also add to the remarks I have made, for I am not going to enter at large upon this subject, that I have never had the least apprehension that I or my friends would marry negroes if there was no law to keep them from it.* [Laughter] *But as Judge Douglas and his friends seem to be in great apprehension that they might, if there were no law to keep them from it* [roars of laughter], *I give him the most solemn pledge that I will to the very last stand by the law of this state which forbids the marrying of white people with negroes.* [Continued laughter and applause.]

Lincoln's racial attitudes have been the subject of much debate among scholars. Some believe that Lincoln, like Douglas, dreamed of a white man's country and consider his early commitment to Henry Clay's colonization scheme—sending the slaves "back" to Africa—tantamount to ethnic cleansing. Others emphasize the degree to which Lincoln "evolved" on the issue of race—so much so that his final speech, in support of black suffrage, may have gotten him killed. (Listening to the speech, John Wilkes Booth was reported to have said: "That means n---r citizenship. Now, by God, I'll put him through. That is the last speech he will ever make." How does Lincoln handle race here? What do you think were his real views? What do you make of his use of humor? Was it effective?

Douglas: Mr. Lincoln said that he was not in favor of the social and political equality of the negro with the white man. Everywhere up North he has declared that he was not in favor of the social and political equality of the negro, but he would not say whether or not he was opposed to negroes voting and negro citizenship. I want to know whether he is for or against negro citizenship? He declared his utter opposition to the Dred Scott decision, and advanced as a reason that the Court had decided that it was not possible for a negro to be a citizen under the Constitution of the United States. If he is opposed to the Dred Scott decision for that reason, he must be in favor of conferring the right and privilege of citizenship upon the negro! I have been trying to get an answer from him on that point, but have never yet obtained one, and I will show you why. In every speech he made in the North, he quoted the Declaration of Independence to prove that all men were created equal, and insisted that the phrase "all men" included the negro as well as the white man,

and that the equality rested upon Divine law. Here is what he said on
that point:

"I should like to know if taking this old Declaration of Independence, which
declares that all men are equal upon principle, and making exceptions to it
where will it stop. If one man says it does not mean a negro, why may not another say it does not mean some other man? If that declaration is not the
truth, let us get the statute book in which we find it, and tear it out!"

Lincoln maintains there that the Declaration of Independence asserts that
the negro is equal to the white man, and that under divine law, and if he believes so, it was rational for him to advocate negro citizenship, which, when
allowed, puts the negro on an equality under the law. I say to you in all frank-
ness, gentlemen, that in my opinion a negro is not a citizen, cannot be, and
ought not to be, under the Constitution of the United States. I will not even
qualify my opinion to meet the declaration of one of the judges of the
Supreme Court in the Dred Scott case, that a negro descended from African
parents, who was imported into this country as a slave is not a citizen, and
cannot be. I say that this government was established on the white basis. It
was made by white men, for the benefit of white men and their posterity forever, and never should be administered by any except white men. [Cheers.]
I declare that a negro ought not to be a citizen, whether his parents were imported into this country as slaves or not, or whether or not he was born here. It
does not depend upon the place a negro's parents were born, or whether they
were slaves or not, but upon the fact that he is a negro, belonging to a race
incapable of self-government, and for that reason ought not to be on an equality with white men. [Immense applause.]

Lincoln: Judge Douglas has said to you that he has not been able to get
from me an answer to the question whether I am in favor of negro citizenship.
So far as I know, the Judge never asked me the question before. [Applause.]
He shall have no occasion to ever ask it again, for I tell him very frankly that I
am not in favor of negro citizenship. [Renewed applause.] This furnishes me
an occasion for saying a few words upon the subject. I mentioned in a certain
speech of mine which has been printed, that the Supreme Court had decided
that a negro could not possibly be made a citizen, and without saying what
was my ground of complaint in regard to that, or whether I had any ground of
complaint, Judge Douglas has from that thing manufactured nearly every
thing that he ever says about my disposition to produce an equality between
the negroes and the white people. [Laughter, applause.] If any one will read
my speech, he will find I mentioned that as one of the points decided in the
course of the Supreme Court opinions, but I did not state what objection I had
to it. But Judge Douglas tells the people what my objection was when I did not
tell them myself. [Applause, laughter.] Now my opinion is that the different
States have the power to make a negro a citizen under the Constitution of the
United States if they choose. The Dred Scott decision decides that they have

not that power. If the State of Illinois had that power I should be opposed to the exercise of it. [Cries of "Good," "good," and applause.] *That is all I have to say about it.*

Judge Douglas has told me that he heard my speeches north and my speeches south, that he had heard me at Ottawa and at Freeport in the north, and recently at Jonesboro in the south, and there was a very different cast of sentiment in the speeches made at the different points. I will not charge upon Judge Douglas that he willfully misrepresents me, but I call upon every fair-minded man to take these speeches and read them, and I dare him to point out any difference between my speeches north and south. [Great cheering.]

When Judge Trumbull, our other Senator in Congress, returned to Illinois in the month of August, he made a speech at Chicago, in which he made what may be called a charge *against Judge Douglas, which I understand* proved *to be very offensive to him. Trumbull's charge is in the following words: "that there was a plot entered into to have a Constitution formed for Kansas, and put in force, without giving the people an opportunity to vote upon it, and that Mr. Douglas was in the plot."*

[The critical section of the original Toombs bill, according to Trumbull] is in these words:

"That the following propositions be and the same are hereby offered to the said Convention of the people of Kansas when formed, for their free acceptance or rejection; which, if accepted by the Convention and ratified by the people at the election for the adoption of the Constitution, *shall be obligatory upon the United States and the said State of Kansas."*

Now, Trumbull alleges that these last words were stricken out of the bill when it came back. The point upon Judge Douglas is this. The bill that went into his hands had the provision in it for a submission of the constitution to the people. And I say its language amounts to an express provision for a submission, and that he took the provision out. And now, my direct question to Judge Douglas is, to answer why he found it necessary to strike out those particular harmless words. I ask him whether he took the original provision out, which Trumbull alleges was in the bill? If he admits that he did take it, I ask him what he did for it? *It looks to us as if he had altered the bill. If it looks differently to him—if he has a different reason for his action from the one we assign him—*he can tell it. *I insist upon knowing why he made the bill silent upon that point, when it was vocal before he put his hands upon it.*

Douglas: *Ladies and gentlemen: I had* supposed *that we assembled here today for the purpose of a joint discussion between Mr. Lincoln and myself upon the political questions that now agitate the whole country. Let me ask you what question of public policy, relating to the welfare of this state or the Union, has Mr. Lincoln discussed before you?* [Cries of 'None, none,' and great applause.] *Gentlemen, allow me to suggest that silence is the best compliment you can pay me. I need my whole time, and your cheering only occupies it.*

I wish you to bear in mind that up to the time of the introduction of the Toombs bill, and after its introduction, there had never been an act of Congress for the admission of a new state which contained a clause requiring its constitution to be submitted to the people. The general rule made the law silent on the subject, taking it for granted that the people would demand and compel a popular vote on the ratification of their constitution. Such was the general rule under Washington, Jefferson, Madison, Jackson and Polk, under the Whig Presidents and the Democratic Presidents from the beginning of the Government down, and nobody dreamed that an effort would ever be made to abuse the power thus confided to the people of a territory. For this reason our attention was not called to the fact of whether there was or was not a clause in the Toombs bill compelling submission, but it was taken for granted that the constitution would be submitted to the people whether the law compelled it or not.

In my report accompanying the Toombs bill, I said: "In the opinion of your committee, whenever a constitution shall be formed in any territory, preparatory to its admission into the Union as a state, justice, the genius of our institutions, the whole theory of our republican system imperatively demand that the voice of the people shall be fairly expressed, and their will embodied in that fundamental law, without fraud or violence, or intimidation, or any other improper or unlawful influence, and subject to no other restrictions than those imposed by the Constitution of the United States." [Cheers.]

There you find that we took it for granted that the constitution was to be submitted to the people, whether the bill was silent on the subject or not. I ask you to reflect on these things, for I tell you that there is a conspiracy to carry this election for the Black Republicans by slander, and not by fair means. Mr. Lincoln's speech this day is conclusive evidence of the fact. He has devoted his time to an issue between Mr. Trumbull and myself and has not uttered a word about the politics of the day. Are you going to elect Mr. Trumbull's colleague upon an issue between Mr. Trumbull and me? [Laughter and cheers.] I thought I was running against Abraham Lincoln, that he claimed to be my opponent, and challenged me to a discussion of the public questions of the day with him, and was discussing these questions with me. But it turns out that his only hope is to ride into office on Trumbull's back, who will carry him by falsehood. [Cheers.]

Permit me to pursue this subject a little further. An examination of the record proves that Trumbull's charge—that the Toombs bill originally contained a clause requiring the Constitution to be submitted to the people—is false. The printed copy of the bill which Mr. Lincoln held up before you, and which he pretends contains such a clause—there is no clause in it requiring a submission of the constitution. Mr. Lincoln cannot find such a clause in it. There never was a clause in the Toombs bill requiring the constitution to be submitted. Trumbull knew it at the time. I read from Trumbull's speech in the Senate on the Toombs bill on the night of its passage.

I [therefore] repeat my charge that Trumbull did falsify the public records of the country, in order to make his charge against me. [Cheers, applause.] And I tell Mr. Abraham Lincoln that if he will examine these records, he will then know that what I state is true. Mr. Lincoln has this day indorsed Mr. Trumbull's veracity after he had my word for it that that veracity was proved to be violated and forfeited by the public records. It will not do for Mr. Lincoln, in parading his calumnies against me, to put Mr. Trumbull between him and the odium and responsibility which justly attaches to such calumnies. I tell him that I am as ready to prosecute the endorser as the maker of a forged note. [Cheers, applause.]

I regret the necessity of occupying my time with these petty personal matters. It is unbecoming the dignity of a canvass for an office of the character for which we are candidates. When I commenced the canvass at Chicago, I spoke of Mr. Lincoln in terms of kindness as an old friend. I said that he was a good citizen, of unblemished character, against whom I had nothing to say. I repeated these complimentary remarks about him in my successive speeches, until he became the endorser for these and other slanders against me. If there is any thing personally disagreeable, uncourteous or disreputable in these personalities, the sole responsibility rests on Mr. Lincoln, Mr. Trumbull, and their backers.

Lincoln: *The Judge thinks it is altogether wrong that I should have dwelt upon this charge of Trumbull's at all.*

I ask the attention of this audience to the question whether I have succeeded in sustaining the charge ["Yes," "yes"], *and whether Judge Douglas has at all succeeded in rebutting it?* [Loud cries of "No, no."] *Does he say that what I present here as a copy of the original Toombs bill is a forgery?* ["No," "no."] *Does he say that what I present as a copy of the bill reported by himself is a forgery?* ["No," "no," "no."] *Or what is presented as a transcript from the Globe is a forgery?* ["No," "no," "no."] *Does he say the quotations from his own speech are forgeries?* ["No," "no," "no."] *Does he say this transcript from Trumbull's speech is a forgery?* [Loud cries of "No, no." "He didn't deny one of them."] I would then like to know how it comes about that when each piece of a story is true, the whole story turns out false? [Great cheers and laughter.] *I take it these people have some sense. They see plainly that Judge Douglas is playing cuttlefish* [laughter], *a small species of fish that has no mode of defending itself when pursued except by throwing out a black fluid, which makes the water so dark the enemy cannot see it and thus it escapes.* [Roars of laughter.] *Ain't the Judge playing the cuttlefish?* ["Yes, yes," and cheers.]

In regard to Trumbull's charge that he, Douglas, [struck out] a provision [of] the bill to prevent the constitution being submitted to the people, what is his answer? I assert that you [pointing to an individual], *are here today, and you undertake to prove me a liar by showing that you were in Mattoon yesterday.* [Laughter.] *I say that you took your hat off your head, and you prove me a liar by putting it on your head. [Roars of laughter.] That is the whole force of Douglas's argument.*

Now, I want to come back to my original question. Trumbull says that Judge Douglas had a bill with a provision in it for submitting a constitution to be made to a vote of the people of Kansas. Does Judge Douglas deny that fact? [Cries of "No, no."] Does he deny that the provision which Trumbull reads was put in that bill? ["No, no."] Then Trumbull says he struck it out. Does he have to deny that? ["No," "no," "no."] He does not, and I have the right to repeat the question—why Judge Douglas took it out? [Immense applause.]

Now I ask what is the reason Judge Douglas is so chary about coming to the exact question? What is the reason he will not tell you any thing about how it was made, by whom it was made, or that he remembers it being made at all? Why does he stand playing upon the meaning of words, and quibbling around the edges of the evidence? If he can explain all this, but leaves it unexplained, I have a right to infer that Judge Douglas understood it was the purpose of his party, in engineering that bill through, to make a Constitution, and have Kansas come into the Union with that constitution, without its being sub-mitted to a vote of the people. *["That's it."] Until he gives a better or more plausible reason than he has offered against the evidence in the case,* I suggest to him it will not avail him at all that he swells himself up, takes on dignity, and calls people liars. *[Great applause and laughter.]*

Why, sir, there is not a word in Trumbull's speech that depends on Trumbull's veracity at all. He has only arrayed the evidence and told you what follows as a matter of reasoning. There is not a statement in the whole speech that depends on Trumbull's word. If you have ever studied geometry, you remember that by a course of reasoning, Euclid proves that all the angles in a triangle are equal to two right angles. Euclid has shown you how to work it out. Now, if you undertake to disprove that proposition, and to show that it is erroneous, would you prove it to be false by calling Euclid a liar? [Roars of laughter and enthusiastic cheers.]

Lincoln spends a significant amount of time during this debate on the offensive, attacking Douglas for (apparently) striking a clause from a bill before his committee. Can such highly specific charges make good political theater? Is there some substance behind the charge too?

Douglas: *Fellow citizens, I came here for the purpose of discussing the leading political topics which now agitate the country. I have no charges to make*

against Mr. Lincoln, none against Mr. Trumbull, and none against any man who is a candidate, except in repelling their assaults upon me. If Mr. Lincoln is a man of bad character, I leave you to find it out. If his votes in the past are not satisfactory, I leave others to ascertain the fact. If his course on the Mexican war was not in accordance with your notions of patriotism and fidelity to our own country as against a public enemy, I leave you to ascertain the fact. I have no assaults to make upon him except to trace his course on the questions that now divide the country and engross so much of the people's attention.

My friends, I am sorry that I have not time to pursue this argument further, as I might have done but for the fact that Mr. Lincoln compelled me to occupy a portion of my time in repelling those gross slanders and falsehoods that Trumbull has invented against me and put in circulation. In conclusion, let me ask you why should this Government be divided by a geographical line— *arraying all men North in one great hostile party against all men South? Why cannot this government endure divided into free and slave states, as our fathers made it? Why can we not thus continue to prosper? We can if we will live up to and execute the government upon those principles upon which our fathers established it. During the whole period of our existence Divine Providence has smiled upon us, and showered upon our nation richer and more abundant blessings than have ever been conferred upon any people on the face of the globe.* [Sustained applause.]

Lincoln: *Judge Douglas complains about a disposition on the part of Trumbull and myself to attack him personally. I want to attend to that suggestion a moment. I don't want to be unjustly accused of dealing illiberally or unfairly with an adversary, either in court, or in a political canvass, or anywhere else. I would despise myself if I supposed myself ready to deal less liberally with an adversary than I was willing to be treated myself. Judge Douglas, in a general way, without putting it in a direct shape, revives the old charge against me in reference to the Mexican War. He does not take the responsibility of putting it in a very definite form, but makes a general reference to it. That charge is more than ten years old. He complains of Trumbull and myself, because he says we bring charges against him one or two years old. He knows, too, that in regard to the Mexican War story, the more respectable papers of his own party throughout the state have been compelled to take it back and acknowledge that it was a lie.* [Continued and vociferous applause.] *He brought this forward at Ottawa, the first time we met face to face; and in the opening speech that Judge Douglas made, he attacked me in regard to a matter ten years old. Isn't he a pretty man to be whining about people making charges against him only two years old.* [Cheers.]

While I am here perhaps I ought to say a word, if I have the time, in regard to the latter portion of the Judge's speech, which was a sort of declamation in reference to my having said I entertained the belief that this Government would not endure, half slave and half free. Now at this day in the history of the world we can no more foretell where the end of this slavery agitation will be than we can see the end of the world itself. The Nebraska–Kansas bill was introduced four years and a half ago, and if the agitation is ever to come to an end, we may say we are four years and a half nearer the end. So, too, we can say we are four years and a half nearer the end of the world, and we can just as clearly see the end of the world as we can see the end of this agitation. [Applause.] The Kansas settlement did not conclude it. If Kansas should sink today and leave a great vacant space in the earth's surface, this vexed question would still be among us. I say, then, there is no way of putting an end to the slavery agitation amongst us but to put it back upon the basis where our fathers placed it [applause], no way but to keep it out of our new territories [renewed applause], to restrict it forever to the old states where it now exists. [Tremendous and prolonged cheering; cries of "That's the doctrine," "good," "good," &c.] Then the public mind will rest in the belief that it is in the course of ultimate extinction. That is one way of putting an end to the slavery agitation. [Applause.]

The other way is for us to surrender and let Judge Douglas and his friends have their way and plant slavery over all the states, cease speaking of it as in any way a wrong, regard slavery as one of the common matters of property, and speak of negroes as we do of our horses and cattle. But while it drives on in its state of progress as it is now driving, and as it has driven for the last five years, I have ventured the opinion, and I say today, that we will have no end to the slavery agitation until it takes one turn or the other. [Applause.]

CHAPTER 5

Fifth Debate, Galesburg, Illinois, October 7, 1858

Although geographically situated in the center-west of the state, Galesburg, Illinois, was a Republican stronghold. Founded in 1835 by New York Presbyterian George Washington Gale as the site of a manual labor college (now Knox College), Galesburg was home to one of the earliest antislavery societies in Illinois and was a common stop on the Underground Railroad. The Galesburg crowd, which probably numbered about 15,000, would be the most hostile Douglas had faced since Freeport, and his tireless stumping and speechifying had so worn down his voice that he was probably only heard by a third of the audience. The weather too had turned, and a whipping, chill wind forced the local arrangements committee to move the stage from the exposed town square to the leeward side of a three-storied classroom building on the Knox campus. (Douglas and Lincoln would mount the rostrum by going through the building and up a flight of stairs to get to the stage via a convenient window.)

Douglas: *Ladies and Gentlemen: At Charleston [Lincoln] defied me to show that there was any difference between his speeches in the North and in the South [of the state]. I will now call your attention to two of them, and you can then say whether you would be apt to believe that the same man ever uttered both. [Laughter and cheers.] In a speech in reply to me at Chicago in July last, Mr. Lincoln, in speaking of the equality of the negro with the white man, used the following language:*

"I should like to know, if taking this old Declaration of Independence, which declares that all men are equal upon principle, and making exceptions to it, where will it stop? If one man says it does not mean a negro, why may not another man say it does not mean another man? If that declaration is not the truth, let us get the statute book in which we find it and tear it out! Who is so bold as to do it? If it is not true let us tear it out!"

You find that Mr. Lincoln there proposed that if the doctrine of the Declaration of Independence, declaring all men to be born equal, did not include the negro and put him on an equality with the white man, that we should take the statute book and tear it out. [Laughter and cheers.]

[Now] I will show you in immediate contrast with that doctrine, what Mr. Lincoln said down in Egypt in order to get votes in that locality, where they do not hold to such a doctrine. [Applause.] In a joint discussion between Mr. Lincoln and myself, at Charleston, I think, on the 18th of last month, Mr. Lincoln, referring to this subject, used the following language:

"I will say then, that I am not nor never have been in favor of bringing about in any way the social and political equality of the white and black races; that I am not nor never have been in favor of making voters of the free negroes, or jurors, or qualifying them to hold office, or having them to marry with white people. I will say in addition, that there is a physical difference between the white and black races, which, I suppose, will forever forbid the two races living together upon terms of social and political equality, and inasmuch as they cannot so live, that while they do remain together, there must be the position of superior and inferior, that I as much as any other man am in favor of the superior position being assigned to the white man."

Now, how can you reconcile those two positions of Mr. Lincoln?

I tell you that this Chicago doctrine of Lincoln's—declaring that the negro and the white man are made equal by the Declaration of Independence and by Divine Providence—is a monstrous heresy. [Applause.] The signers of the Declaration of Independence never dreamed of the negro when they were writing that document. They referred to white men, to men of European birth and European descent, when they declared the equality of all men. I see a gentleman there in the crowd shaking his head. Let me remind him that when Thomas Jefferson wrote that document, he was the owner, and so continued until his death, of a large number of slaves. Did he intend to say in that Declaration, that his negro slaves, which he held and treated as property, were created his equals by Divine law, and that he was violating the law of God every day of his life by holding them as slaves? It must be borne in mind that when that Declaration was put forth, every one of the thirteen Colonies were slaveholding Colonies, and every man who signed that instrument represented a slaveholding constituency. Recollect, also, that no one of them emancipated his slaves, much less put them on an equality with himself, after he signed the Declaration. On the contrary, they all continued to hold their negroes as slaves during the Revolutionary War. Now, do you believe—are you willing to have it said—that every man who signed the Declaration of Independence declared the negro his equal, and then was hypocrite enough to continue to hold him as a slave, in violation of what he believed to be the divine law? [Cries of "No!"] And yet when you say that the Declaration of Independence includes the negro, you charge the signers of it with hypocrisy.

Lincoln: The Judge has alluded to the Declaration of Independence, and insisted that negroes are not included in that Declaration, and that it is a slander upon the framers of that instrument to suppose that negroes were meant therein. And he asks you: Is it possible to believe that Mr. Jefferson, who penned the immortal paper, could have supposed himself applying the language of that instrument to the negro race, and yet have held a portion of that race in slavery? Would he not at once have freed them? I only have to remark upon this part of the Judge's speech—and that, too, very briefly, for I shall not detain myself, or you, upon that point for any great length of time—that I believe the entire records of the world, from the date of the Declaration of Independence up to within three years ago, may be searched in vain for one single affirmation, from one single man, that the negro was not included in the Declaration of Independence. I think I may defy Judge Douglas to show that he ever said so, that Washington ever said so, that any president ever said so, that any member of Congress ever said so, or that any living man upon the whole earth ever said so, until the necessities of the present policy of the Democratic party, in regard to slavery, had to invent that affirmation. [Applause.] And I will remind Judge Douglas and this audience, that while Mr. Jefferson was the owner of slaves, as undoubtedly he was, in speaking upon this very subject, he used the strong language that he trembled for his country when he remembered that God was just. And I will offer the highest premium in my power to Judge Douglas if he will show that he, in all his life, ever uttered a sentiment at all akin to that of Jefferson. [Applause and cheers.]

Now a few words in regard to these extracts from speeches of mine, which Judge Douglas has read to you and which he supposes are in very great contrast to each other. Those speeches have been before the public for a considerable time, and if they have any inconsistency in them, if there is any conflict in them, the public have been unable to detect it. When the Judge says, in speaking on this subject, that I make speeches of one sort for the people of the northern end of the state, and of a different sort for the southern people, he assumes that I do not understand that my speeches will be put in print and read north and south. I knew all the while that the speech that I made at Chicago, and the one I made at Jonesboro, and the one at Charleston, would all be put in print, and all the reading and intelligent men in the community would see them and know all about my opinions. And I have not supposed, and do not now suppose, that there is any conflict whatever between them. [Cheers.]

Douglas: My point of complaint against him is that I cannot induce him to hold up the same standard, to carry the same flag in all parts of the state. He does not pretend, and no other man will, that I have one set of principles for Galesburg and another for Charleston. ["No. no."] He does not pretend that I hold to one doctrine in Chicago and an opposite one in Jonesboro. I have proved that he has a different set of principles for each of these localities. [Cries of opposition.] Silence, if you please. All I asked of him was that he should deliver the speech that he has made here today in Coles County instead

*of in old Knox. It would have settled the question between us in that doubtful
county, if the speech delivered here had been made there. Here I understand
him to reaffirm the doctrine of negro equality, and to assert that, by the
Declaration of Independence, the negro is declared equal to the white man.
He tells you today that the negro was included in the Declaration of Independence when it asserted that all men were created equal. ["We believe it."] You
believe it. Very well.*

[Here an uproar arose, with people throughout the crowd groaning,
cheering, and making cat calls and other noises, preventing the speaker
from proceeding.]

Douglas: *Gentlemen, I ask you to remember that Mr. Lincoln was listened
to respectfully, and I have the right to insist that I shall not be interrupted
during my reply.*

Lincoln: *I hope that silence will be preserved.*

Douglas: *Mr. Lincoln asserts today, as he did at Chicago, that the negro
was included in that clause of the Declaration of Independence which says
that all men were created equal and endowed by the Creator with certain
inalienable rights, among which are life, liberty, and the pursuit of happiness.
["Ain't that so?"] If the negro was made his equal and mine, if that equality
was established by divine law, and was the negro's inalienable right, how came
he to say at Charleston to the Kentuckians residing in that section of our state,
that the negro was physically inferior to the white man, belonged to an inferior
race, and he was for keeping him always in that inferior condition. ["Good."]
I wish you to bear these things in mind. At Charleston he said that the negro
belonged to an inferior race, and that he was for keeping him in that inferior
condition. There he gave the people to understand that there was no moral
question involved, because the inferiority being established, it was only a question of degree and not a question of right. Here today, instead of making it a
question of degree, he makes it a moral question, says that it is a great crime
to hold the negro in that inferior condition. ["He's right."] Is he right now or
was he right in Charleston? ["Both."] He is right then, sir, in your estimation,
not because he is consistent, but because he can trim his principles any way in
any section, so as to secure votes. All I desire of him is that he will declare the
same principles in the south that he does in the north.*

Lincoln: *I have never manifested any impatience with the necessities that
spring from the actual presence of black people amongst us, and the actual
existence of slavery amongst us where it does already exist. But I have insisted
that, in legislating for new countries, where it does not exist, there is no just
rule other than that of moral and abstract right! With reference to those new
countries, those maxims as to the right of a people to "life, liberty and the pursuit of happiness," were the just rules to be constantly referred to. There is no
misunderstanding this, except by men interested to misunderstand it.*
[Applause.]

Douglas: *But Mr. Lincoln cannot be made to understand, and those who are determined to vote for him, no matter whether he is a pro-slavery man in the south and a negro equality advocate in the north, cannot be made to understand how it is that in a territory the people can do as they please on the slavery question under the Dred Scott decision. [The Republican party] is unlike all other political organizations in this country. All other parties have been national in their character, have avowed their principles alike in the slave and free States, in Kentucky as well as Illinois, in Louisiana as well as in Massachusetts. Such was the case with the old Whig party, and such was and is the case with the Democratic party. Whigs and Democrats could proclaim their principles boldly and fearlessly in the North and in the South, in the East and in the West, wherever the Constitution ruled and the American flag waved over American soil.*

But now you have a sectional organization, a party which appeals to the Northern section of the Union against the Southern, a party which appeals to Northern passion, Northern pride, Northern ambition, and Northern prejudices, against Southern people, the Southern States, and Southern institutions. The leaders of that party hope that they will be able to unite the Northern states in one great sectional party, and inasmuch as the North is the strongest section, that they will thus be enabled to out-vote, conquer, govern, and control the South. Hence you find that they now make speeches advocating principles and measures which cannot be defended in any slaveholding state of this Union. Is there a Republican residing in Galesburg who can travel into Kentucky and carry his principles with him across the Ohio? ["No."] What Republican from Massachusetts can visit the Old Dominion without leaving his principles behind him when he crosses Mason and Dixon's line? Permit me to say to you in perfect good humor, but in all sincerity, that no political creed is sound which cannot be proclaimed fearlessly in every state of this Union where the federal Constitution is not the supreme law of the land. ["That's so," and cheers.]

Lincoln: *The Judge has detained us awhile in regard to the distinction between his party and our party. His he assumes to be a national party, ours, a sectional one. He does this in asking the question whether this country has any interest in the maintenance of the Republican party? He assumes that our party is altogether sectional—that the party to which he adheres is national. And the argument is, that no party can be a rightful party, can be based upon rightful principles, unless it can announce its principles every where. Now, it is the first time, I believe, that I have ever heard it announced as being true, that a man could always announce rightful principles everywhere! I presume that Judge Douglas could not go into Russia and announce the doctrine of our national democracy. He could not denounce the doctrine of kings and emperors and monarchies in Russia. And it may be true of this country, that in some places we may not be able to proclaim a doctrine as clearly true as the truth of democracy, because there is a section so directly opposed to it that they will not tolerate us in doing so. Is it the true test of the soundness of a doctrine, that in some places people won't let you proclaim it? Is that the way to test the truth of any doctrine?*

Douglas: *Did you notice how he answered my position that a man should hold the same doctrines throughout the length and breadth of this republic? He said, "Would Judge Douglas go to Russia and proclaim the same principles he does here?" I would remind him that Russia is not under the American Constitution.* ["Good," and laughter.] *If Russia was a part of the American republic, under our federal Constitution, and I was sworn to support the Constitution, I would maintain the same doctrine in Russia that I do in Illinois.* [Cheers.] *The slaveholding states are governed by the same federal Constitution as ourselves, and hence a man's principles, in order to be in harmony with the Constitution, must be the same in the South as they are in the North, the same in the free states as they are in the slave states. Whenever a man advocates one set of principles in one section, and another set in another section, his opinions are in violation of the spirit of the Constitution which he has sworn to support.* ["That's so."] *When Mr. Lincoln went to Congress in 1847, and laying his hand upon the holy evangelists, made a solemn vow in the presence of high heaven that he would be faithful to the Constitution, what did he mean? The Constitution as he expounds it in Galesburg, or the Constitution as he expounds it in Charleston.* [Cheers.]

Lincoln: *I suppose that the real difference between Judge Douglas and his friends, and the Republicans on the contrary, is that the Judge is not in favor of making any difference between slavery and liberty, that he is in favor of eradicating, of pressing out of view, the questions of preference in this country for free or slave institutions. And consequently every sentiment he utters discards the idea that there is any wrong in slavery. Everything that emanates from him or his coadjutors in their course of policy carefully excludes the thought that there is any thing wrong in slavery. All their arguments, if you will consider them, will be seen to exclude the thought that there is any thing whatever wrong in slavery. If you will take the Judge's speeches, and select the short and pointed sentences expressed by him—as his declaration that he "don't care whether slavery is voted up or down"—you will see at once that this is perfectly logical, if you do not admit that slavery is wrong. If you do admit that it is wrong, Judge Douglas cannot logically say he don't care whether a wrong is voted up or voted down. Judge Douglas declares that if any community want slavery they have a right to have it. He can say that logically, if he says that there is no wrong in slavery. But if you admit that there is a wrong in it, he cannot logically say that any body has a right to do wrong. He insists that, upon the score of equality, the owners of slaves and owners of property— of horses and every other sort of property—should be alike and hold them alike in a new territory. That is perfectly logical if the two species of property are alike and are equally founded in right.*

But if you admit that one of them is wrong, you cannot institute any equality between right and wrong. And from this difference of sentiment—the belief on the part of one that the institution is wrong, and a policy springing from that belief which looks to the arrest of the enlargement of that wrong; and this other sentiment, that it is no wrong, and a policy springing from that sentiment which will tolerate no idea of preventing that wrong from growing larger, and looks to there never being an end of it through all the existence of things—arises the real difference between Judge Douglas and his friends, on the one hand, and the Republicans on the other.

Douglas: Let us see whether I cannot explain [this] to the satisfaction of all impartial men. Chief Justice Taney has said in his opinion in the Dred Scott case, that a negro slave, being property, stands on an equal footing with other property, and that the owner may carry them into United States territory the same as he does other property. Suppose any two of you, neighbors, should conclude to go to Kansas, one carrying $100,000 worth of negro slaves and the other $100,000 worth of mixed merchandise, including quantities of liquors. You both agree that under that decision you may carry your property to Kansas, but when you get it there, the merchant who is possessed of the liquors is met by the Maine liquor law, which prohibits the sale or use of his property, and the owner of the slaves is met by equally unfriendly legislation, which makes his property worthless after he gets it there. What is the right to carry your property into the territory worth to either, when unfriendly legislation in the territory renders it worthless after you get it there? The slaveholder, when he gets his slaves there, finds that there is no local law to protect him in holding them, no slave code, no police regulation maintaining and supporting him in his right, and he discovers at once that the absence of such friendly legislation excludes his property from the territory, just as irresistibly as if there was a positive constitutional prohibition excluding it. Thus you find it is with any kind of property in a territory; it depends for its protection on the local and municipal law. If the people of a territory want slavery, they make friendly legislation to introduce it, but if they do not want it, they withhold all protection from it, and then it cannot exist there. I hold that in this country there is no power, there should be no power on the face of the globe, that can force any institution on an unwilling people. The great fundamental principle of our government is that the people of each state and each territory shall be left perfectly free to decide for themselves what shall be the nature and character of their institutions.

Lincoln: The essence of the Dred Scott case is compressed into the sentence which I will now read: "Now, as we have already said in an earlier part of this opinion, upon a different point, the right of property in a slave is distinctly and expressly affirmed in the Constitution." I repeat it, "The right of property in a slave is distinctly and expressly affirmed in the Constitution!" What is [it to be] affirmed in the Constitution? Made firm in the Constitution, so made *that it cannot be separated from the Constitution without breaking the Constitution, durable as the Constitution, and part of the Constitution. Now, remembering the provision of the Constitution which I have read, affirming that that instrument is the supreme law of the land, that the judges of every state shall be bound by it, any law or constitution of any state to the contrary notwithstanding, that the right of property in a slave is affirmed in that Constitution, is made firm in it, and cannot be separated from it without breaking it, durable as the instrument, part of the instrument, what follows as a short and even syllogistic argument from it? I think it follows, and I submit to the consideration of men capable of arguing, whether, as I state it in syllogistic form, the argument has any fault in it:*

Nothing in the constitution or laws of any state can destroy a right distinctly and expressly affirmed in the Constitution of the United States.

The right of property in a slave is distinctly and expressly affirmed in the Constitution of the United States.

Therefore, nothing in the constitution or laws of any state can destroy the right of property in a slave.

I believe that no fault can be pointed out in that argument. Assuming the truth of the premises, the conclusion, so far as I have capacity at all to understand it, follows inevitably.

There is a fault in it, as I think, but the fault is not in the reasoning, but the fault is the falsehood in fact of one of the premises. I believe that the right of property in a slave is not distinctly and expressly affirmed in the Constitution, and Judge Douglas thinks it is. I believe that the Supreme Court and the advocates of that decision may search in vain for the place in the Constitution where the right of a slave is distinctly and expressly affirmed. I say, therefore, that I think one of the premises is not true in fact. This is but an opinion, and the opinion of one very humble man. But it is my opinion that the Dred Scott decision, as it is, never would have been made in its present form if the party that made it had not been sustained previously by the elections. My own opinion is, that the new Dred Scott decision, deciding against the right of the people of the states to exclude slavery, will never be made, if that party is not sustained by the elections. [Cheers.] I believe, further, that it is just as sure to be made as tomorrow is to come, if that party shall be sustained. [Cheers.] I have said, upon a former occasion, and I repeat it now, that the course of argument that Judge Douglas makes use of upon this subject—I charge not his motives in this—is preparing the public mind for the new Dred Scott decision. Jefferson said, that "judges are as honest as other men, and not more so." And he said, substantially, that "whenever a free people should give up in absolute submission to any department of government, retaining for themselves no appeal from it, their liberties were gone."

Lincoln was not a broad reader but a deep one. He tended to pore over the same books again and again. "I am slow to learn and slow to forget," he told a friend. "My mind is like a piece of steel, very hard to scratch any thing on it and almost impossible after you get it there to rub it out." It makes sense that Lincoln would often quote Henry Clay, the political idol of his early years. But does it surprise you how often he quotes Thomas Jefferson, a Southerner and a slaveholder? Who else does Lincoln quote often? Does Douglas quote specific people? Do you think what someone reads (and quotes) shapes who they are? Or reveals something about them?

So far in this controversy I can get no answer at all from Judge Douglas upon these subjects. Not one can I get from him, except that he swells himself up and says, "All of us who stand by the decision of the Supreme Court are the friends of the Constitution; all you fellows that dare question it in any way, are the enemies of the Constitution." [Laughter, cheers.] And the manner in which he adheres to it—not as being right upon the merits, as he conceives, because he did not discuss that at all, but as being absolutely obligatory upon everyone simply because of the source from whence it comes, as that which no man can gainsay, whatever it may be—this is another marked feature of his adherence to that decision. It marks it in this respect, that it commits him to the next decision, whenever it comes, as being as obligatory as this one. Since he does not investigate it, and won't inquire whether this opinion is right or wrong, so he takes the next one without inquiring whether it is right or wrong. [Applause.] He teaches men this doctrine, and in so doing prepares the public mind to take the next decision when it comes, without any inquiry. In this I think I argue fairly, without questioning motives at all, that Judge Douglas is more ingeniously and powerfully preparing the public mind to take that decision when it comes.

And not only so, but he is doing it in various other ways. In these general maxims about liberty, in his assertions that he don't care whether slavery is voted up or voted down, that whoever wants slavery has a right to have it, that upon principles of equality it should be allowed to go everywhere, that there is no inconsistency between free and slave institutions. In this he is also preparing, whether purposely or not, the way for making the institution of slavery national! [Cheers.] I repeat again, for I wish no misunderstanding, that I do not charge that he means it so. But I call upon your minds to inquire: if you were going to get the best instrument you could, and then set it to work in the most ingenious way, to prepare the public mind for this movement, operating in the free states where there is now an abhorrence of the institution of slavery, could you find an instrument so capable of doing it as Judge Douglas?

I have said once before, and I will repeat it now, that Mr. Clay, when he was once answering an objection to the Colonization Society, that it had a tendency to the ultimate emancipation of the slaves, said that those who would repress all tendencies to liberty and ultimate emancipation must do more than put down the benevolent efforts of the Colonization Society. They must go back to the era of our liberty and independence, and muzzle the cannon that thunders its annual joyous return; they must blot out the moral lights around us; they must penetrate the human soul, and eradicate the light of reason and the love of liberty! And I do think, I repeat, though I said it on a former occasion, that Judge Douglas, and whoever like him teaches that the negro has no share, humble though it may be, in the Declaration of Independence, is going back to the era of our liberty and independence, and, so far as in him lies, muzzling the cannon that thunders its annual joyous return; that he is blowing out the moral lights around us, when he contends that whoever wants slaves has a right to hold them; that he is penetrating, so far as lies in his power, the human soul, and eradicating the light of reason and the love of liberty, when he is in every possible way preparing the public mind, by his vast influence, for making the institution of slavery perpetual and national.
[Applause, cheers.]

Douglas: *Gentlemen: The highest compliment you can pay me during the brief [period] that I have to conclude is by observing a strict silence. I desire to be heard rather than to be applauded.* ["Good."]

I have a few words to say upon the Dred Scott decision, which has troubled the brain of Mr. Lincoln so much. [Laughter.] *Suppose he succeeds in destroying public confidence in the Court, so that the people will not respect its decisions, but will feel at liberty to disregard them, and resist the laws of the land. What will he have gained? He will have changed the government from one of laws into that of a mob, in which the strong arm of violence will be substituted for the decisions of the courts of justice.* ["That's so."]

He complains because I did not go into an argument reviewing Chief Justice Taney's opinion, and the other opinions of the different judges, to determine whether their reasoning is right or wrong on the questions of law. What use would that be? He wants to take an appeal from the Supreme Court to this meeting to determine whether the questions of law were decided properly. He is going to appeal from the Supreme Court of the United States to every town meeting in the hope that he can excite a prejudice against that Court, and on the wave of that prejudice ride into the Senate of the United States, when he could not get there on his own principles, or his own merits. [Laughter and cheers; "hit him again."]

I ask him, whether he is not bound to respect and obey the decisions of the Supreme Court as well as me? The Constitution has created that Court to decide all constitutional questions in the last resort, and when such decisions have been made, they become the law of the land, ["That's so"] *and you, and he, and myself, and every other good citizen are bound by them. Yet, he argues that I am bound by their decisions and he is not. He says that their decisions are binding on Democrats, but not on Republicans. [Laughter and applause.] Are not Republicans bound by the laws of the land as well as Democrats? And when the court has fixed the construction of the Constitution on the validity of a given law, is not their decision binding upon Republicans as well as upon Democrats? ["It ought to be."] Is it possible that you Republicans have the right to raise your mobs and oppose the laws of the land and the constituted authorities, and yet hold us Democrats bound to obey them? My time is within half a minute of expiring, and all I have to say is, that I stand by the laws of the land. ["That's it; "hurrah for Douglas."] I stand by the Constitution as our fathers made it, by the laws as they are enacted, and by the decisions of the court upon all points within their jurisdiction as they are pronounced by the highest tribunal on earth, and any man who resists these must resort to mob law and violence to overturn the government of laws. [Applause.]*

CHAPTER 6

Sixth Debate, Quincy, Illinois, October 13, 1858

Quincy, Illinois, is a Mississippi River town located about a hundred miles due west of Springfield. Although located in the moderate "Whig belt," its close proximity twenty miles upriver from Hannibal, Missouri, made it friendly country for Douglas, a place where many of the Whigs had defected to the Democracy rather than turn Republican. (The district as a whole had voted for Buchanan in 1856.) The weather too had improved, along with Douglas's voice, and October 13 dawned bright and mild for the roughly 12,000 in attendance. Uncharacteristically, Lincoln came out swinging at Quincy and it is clear that by this point in the campaign he had lost patience with the personal tone of some of Douglas's attacks. Douglas too had an uncharacteristic performance, defending poorly and failing to make the most of his "home court" advantage. Part of the problem may have been fatigue. Lincoln was an abstemious man with a high prairie tenor that carried easily, leaving him little fatigued after each debate. Douglas, to use a political "rock star" metaphor had, by the time he made it to Quincy, been out on the road too long, played too many gigs, and spent too many late nights raising his glass to his (declining) health.

✳

Lincoln: *Ladies and gentlemen: I have had no immediate conference with Judge Douglas, but I will venture to say that he and I will perfectly agree that your entire silence, both when I speak and when he speaks, will be most agreeable to us.*

At Jacksonville Judge Douglas made a speech in answer to something said by Judge Trumbull, and at the close of what he said upon that subject, he dared to say that Trumbull had forged his evidence from beginning to end. He said, too, that he should not concern himself with Trumbull any more, but thereafter he should hold Lincoln responsible for the slanders upon him. [Laughter, applause.] When I met him at Charleston after that—although I think that I should not have noticed the subject if he had not said he would hold me responsible for it—I spread out before him the statements of the evidence that Judge Trumbull had used, and I asked Judge Douglas, piece by piece, to put his finger upon one piece of all that evidence that he would say was a forgery! When I went through with each and every piece, Judge Douglas did not dare then to say that any piece of it was a forgery. [Laughter, and cries of "Good, good."] So it seems that there are some things that Judge Douglas dares to do, and some that he dares not to do. [Great applause and laughter.]

A Voice: "It's the same thing with you."

Lincoln: *Yes, sir, it's the same thing with me. I do dare to say forgery when its true, and don't dare to say forgery when it's false. [Thunders of applause. Cries of "Hit him again," "Give it to him, Lincoln."]*

When the Judge says he wouldn't have believed of Abraham Lincoln that he would have made such an attempt as that, he reminds me of the fact that he entered upon this canvass with the purpose to treat me courteously. That touched me somewhat. [Great laughter.] It sets me to thinking. I was aware, when it was first agreed that Judge Douglas and I were to have these seven joint discussions, that they were the successive acts of a drama, perhaps I should say, to be enacted not merely in the face of audiences like this, but in the face of the nation, and to some extent, by my relation to him, and not from any thing in myself, in the face of the world. And I am anxious that they should be conducted with dignity and in the good temper which would be befitting the vast audience before which it was conducted.

Clearly Lincoln understood the importance of these debates in their time. Do you think it would surprise him that we still read them today? Do you think the magnitude of the moment helps explain the pressure both men were under and their occasional flashes of temper? Which debater seems most in control of their emotions?

But in our first discussion at Ottawa, he led off by charging a bargain, some-what corrupt in its character, upon Trumbull and myself—that we had entered into a bargain, one of the terms of which was that Trumbull was to abolitionize the old Democratic party, and I, Lincoln, was to abolitionize the old Whig party, I pretending to be as good an old line Whig as ever. Judge Douglas may not understand that he implicated my truthfulness and my honor, when he said I was doing one thing and pretending another, and I misunderstood him if he thought he was treating me in a dignified way, as a man of honor and truth, as he now claims he was disposed to treat me.

Even after that time, at Galesburg, when he brings forward an extract from a speech made at Chicago, and an extract from a speech made at Charleston, to prove that I was trying to play a double part—that I was trying to cheat the public, and get votes upon one set of principles at one place and upon another set of principles at another place—I do not understand but what he impeaches my honor, my veracity, and my candor. And because he does this, I do not understand that I am bound, if I see a truthful ground for it, to keep my hands off of him.

As soon as I learned that Judge Douglas was disposed to treat me in this way, I signified in one of my speeches that I should be driven to draw upon whatever of humble resources I might have—to adopt a new course with him. I was not entirely sure that I should be able to hold my own with him, but I at least had the purpose made to do as well as I could upon him. And now I say that I will not be the first to cry, "hold." I think it originated with the Judge, and when he quits, I probably will. [Laughter.] But I shall not ask any favors at all. He asks me, or he asks the audience, if I wish to push this matter to the point of personal difficulty.

I tell him, no. He did not make a mistake, in one of his early speeches, when he called me an "amiable" man, though perhaps he did when he called me an "intelligent" man. [Laughter.] It really hurts me very much to suppose that I have wronged any body on earth. I again tell him "no"! I very much prefer, when this canvass shall be over, however it may result, that we at least part without any bitter recollections of personal difficulties.

[But let me get to the point.] There is a sentiment in the country contrary to ours, a sentiment which holds that slavery is not wrong. And therefore it goes for the policy that does not propose dealing with it as a wrong. That policy is the Democratic policy, and that sentiment is the Democratic sentiment. If there be a doubt in the mind of any one of this vast audience that this is really the central idea of the Democratic party, in relation to this subject, I ask him to bear with me while I state a few things tending, as I think, to prove that proposition. In the first place, the leading man—I think I may do my friend Judge Douglas the honor of calling him such—advocating the present Democratic policy, never himself says it is wrong. He has the high distinction, so far as I know, of never having said slavery is either right or wrong. [Laughter.] Almost everybody else says one or the other, but the Judge never does. If there be a man in the Democratic party who thinks it is wrong, and yet clings to that party, I wish him to examine his own course in regard to this matter a moment, and then see if his opinion will not be changed a little. You say it is wrong, but don't you constantly object to any body else saying so? Do you not constantly argue that this is not the right place to oppose it? You say it must not be opposed in the free states, because slavery is not here. It must not be opposed in the slave states, because it is there. It must not be opposed in politics, because that will make a fuss. It must not be opposed in the pulpit, because it is not religion. [Cheers.] Then where is the place to oppose it? There is no place in the country to oppose this evil overspreading the continent, which *you say yourself is coming. Let us understand this. I am not, just here, trying to prove that we are right and they are wrong. I have been stating where we and they stand, and trying to show what is the real difference between us. And I now say that whenever we can get the question distinctly stated—can get all these men who believe that slavery is in some of these respects wrong, to stand and act with us in treating it as a wrong—then, and not till then, I think we will in some way come to an end of this slavery agitation.* [Prolonged cheers.]

Douglas: *Ladies and gentlemen: Permit me to say that unless silence is observed it will be impossible for me to be heard by this immense crowd, and my friends can confer no higher favor upon me than by omitting all expressions of applause or approbation.* ["We cannot help it, Douglas," &c.] *I desire to be heard rather than to be applauded. I wish to address myself to your reason, your judgment, your sense of justice, and not to your passions.*

This Republican organization appeals to the North against the South. It appeals to Northern passion, Northern prejudice, and Northern ambition, against Southern people, Southern States, and Southern institutions, and its only hope of success is by that appeal. Mr. Lincoln thinks that it is his duty to preach a crusade in the free states against slavery because it is a crime, as he believes, and ought to be extinguished, and because the people of the slave states will never abolish it. How is he going to abolish it? Down in the southern part of the state he takes the ground openly that he will not interfere with slavery where it exists, and says that he is not now and never was in favor of interfering with slavery where it exists in the states. Well, if he is not in favor of that, how does he expect to bring slavery in a course of ultimate extinction? How can he extinguish it in Kentucky, in Virginia, in all the slave states by his policy, if he will not pursue a policy which will interfere with it in the states where it exists? Why, he will agitate, he will induce the North to agitate, until the South shall be worried out and forced to abolish slavery.

Let us examine the policy by which that is to be done. He first tells you that he would prohibit slavery everywhere in the territories. He would thus confine slavery within its present limits. When he thus gets it confined, and surrounded, so that it cannot spread, the natural laws of increase will go on until the negroes will be so plenty that they cannot live on the soil. He will hem them in until starvation seizes them, and by starving them to death, he will put slavery in the course of ultimate extinction. If he is not going to interfere with slavery in the states, but intends to interfere and prohibit it in the territories, and thus smother slavery out, it naturally follows, that he can extinguish it only by extinguishing the negro race, for his policy would drive them to starvation. This is the humane and Christian remedy that he proposes for the great crime of slavery.

✳

Here Douglas makes another "parade of horribles" argument in depicting the consequences of locking slavery out of the territories, this time suggesting that Lincoln intended not merely to destroy slavery but the slaves themselves. Why do you think he made this particular argument? And how *did* Lincoln expect slavery to be extinguished in the states where it already existed?

He tells you that I will not argue the question whether slavery is right or wrong. I tell you why I will not do it. I hold that under the Constitution of the United States, each state of this Union has a right to do as it pleases on the subject of slavery. In Illinois we have exercised that sovereign right by prohibiting slavery within our own limits. I approve of that line of policy. We have performed our whole duty in Illinois. We have gone as far as we have a right to go under the Constitution of our common country. It is none of our business whether slavery exists in Missouri or not. Missouri is a sovereign state of this Union, and has the same right to decide the slavery question for herself that Illinois has to decide it for herself. Hence I do not choose to occupy the time allotted to me in discussing a question that we have no right to act upon. I thought that you desired to hear us upon those questions coming within our constitutional power or action. Lincoln will not discuss these. What one question has he discussed that comes within the power or calls for the action or interference of a United States Senator? He is going to discuss the rightfulness of slavery when Congress cannot act upon it either way.

He wishes to discuss the merits of the Dred Scott decision when, under the Constitution, a senator has no right to interfere with the decision of judicial tribunals. He wants your exclusive attention to two questions that he has no power to act upon, to two questions that he could not vote upon if he was in Congress, to two questions that are not practical, in order to conceal your attention from other questions which he might be required to vote upon should he ever become a member of Congress. He tells you that he does not like the Dred Scott decision. Suppose he does not, how is he going to help himself? He says that he will reverse it. How will he reverse it? I know of but one mode of reversing judicial decisions, and that is by appealing from the inferior to the superior court. But I have never yet learned how or where an appeal could be taken from the Supreme Court of the United States! The Dred Scott decision was pronounced by the highest tribunal on earth. From that decision there is no appeal this side of Heaven. Yet, Mr. Lincoln says he is going to reverse that decision. By what tribunal will he reverse it? Will he appeal to a mob? Does he intend to appeal to violence, to Lynch law? Will he stir up strife and rebellion in the land and overthrow the court by violence? He does not deign to tell you how he will reverse the Dred Scott decision, but keeps appealing each day from the Supreme Court of the United States to political meetings in the country. [Laughter.]

He wants me to argue with you the merits of each point of that decision before this political meeting. I say to you, with all due respect, that I choose to abide by the decisions of the Supreme Court as they are pronounced. It is not for me to inquire after a decision is made whether I like it in all the points or not. When I used to practice law with Lincoln, I never knew him to be beat in a case that he did not get mad at the judge and talk about appealing. [Laughter.] And when I got beat I generally thought the court was wrong, but I never dreamed of going out of the court house and making a stump speech to the people against the judge, merely because I had found out that I did not know the law as well as he did. [Laughter.] If the decision did not suit me, I appealed until I got to the Supreme Court, and then if that Court, the highest tribunal in the world, decided against me, I was satisfied, because it is the duty of every law-abiding man to obey the constitutions, the laws, and the consti-tuted authorities. He who attempts to stir up odium and rebellion in the coun-try against the constituted authorities is stimulating the passions of men to resort to violence and to mobs instead of to the law. Hence, I tell you that I take the decisions of the Supreme Court as the law of the land, and I intend to obey them as such.

Lincoln: [Judge Douglas] is desirous of knowing how we are going to reverse the Dred Scott decision. Judge Douglas ought to know how. Did not he and his political friends find a way to reverse the decision of that same court in favor the constitutionality of the National Bank? [Cheers, laughter.] Didn't they find a way to do it so effectually that they have reversed it as completely as any decision ever was reversed, so far as its practical operation is con-cerned? [Cheers.] And let me ask you, didn't Judge Douglas find a way to re-verse the decision of our Supreme Court, when it decided that Carlin's father—old Governor Carlin—had not the constitutional power to remove a Secretary of State? Did he not appeal to the "mobs," as he calls them? Did he not make speeches in the lobby to show how villainous that decision was, and how it ought to be overthrown? Did he not succeed, too, in getting an act passed by the Legislature to have it overthrown? And didn't he himself sit down on that bench as one of the five added judges, who were to overslaugh the four old ones, getting his name of "Judge" in that way and no other? If there is a villainy in using disrespect or making opposition to Supreme Court decisions, I commend it to Judge Douglas's earnest consideration. [Cheers, laughter.] I know of no man in the State of Illinois who ought to know so well about how much villainy it takes to oppose a decision of the Supreme Court as our honorable friend, Stephen A. Douglas. [Applause.]

General Jackson once said each man was bound to support the Constitution "as he understood it." Now, Judge Douglas understands the Constitution ac-cording to the Dred Scott decision, and he is bound to support it as he understands it. I understand it another way, and therefore I am bound to support it in the way in which I understand it. [Applause.]

And as Judge Douglas believes that decision to be correct, does [he] mean to say that the territorial legislature in legislating may, by withholding necessary laws, or by passing unfriendly laws, nullify that constitutional right? Does he mean to say that? Does he mean to ignore the proposition so long and well established in law, that what you cannot do directly, you cannot do indirectly? Does he mean that?

The truth about the matter is this: Judge Douglas has sung paeans to his "popular sovereignty" doctrine until his Supreme Court, cooperating with him, has squatted his "squatter sovereignty" out. [Laughter, applause.] But he will keep up this species of humbuggery about "squatter sovereignty." He has at last invented this sort of "do-nothing sovereignty" [laughter], that the people may exclude slavery by a sort of "sovereignty" that is exercised by doing nothing at all. [Laughter.] Is not that running his "popular sovereignty" down awfully? [Laughter.] Has it not got down as thin as the homeopathic soup that was made by boiling the shadow of a pigeon that had starved to death? [Laughter, cheers.] But at last, when it is brought to the test of close reasoning, there is not even that thin decoction of it left. It is a presumption impossible in the domain of thought. It is precisely no other than the putting of that most unphilosophical proposition, that two bodies can occupy the same space at the same time. The Dred Scott decision covers the whole ground, and while it occupies it, there is no room even for the shadow of a starved pigeon to occupy the same ground. [Great cheering and laughter.]

Douglas: James Buchanan accepted the nomination at Cincinnati on the conditions that the people of a territory, like those of a state, should be left to decide for themselves whether slavery should or should not exist within their limits. I sustained James Buchanan for the presidency on that platform. I will not believe that he has betrayed or intends to betray the platform which elected him. But if he does, I will not follow him. I will stand by that great principle, no matter who may desert it. I intend to stand by it for the purpose of preserving peace between the North and the South, the free and the slave states.

Let each state mind its own business and let its neighbors alone, and there will be no trouble on this question. If we will stand by that principle, then Mr. Lincoln will find that this republic can exist forever divided into free and slave states, as our fathers made it and the people of each state have decided. Stand by that great principle, and we can go on as we have done, increasing in wealth, in population, in power, and in all the elements of greatness, until we shall be the admiration and terror of the world. Under that principle we can receive with entire safety that stream of intelligence which is constantly flowing from the Old World to the New, filling up our prairies, clearing our wildernesses and building cities, towns, railroads and other internal improvements, and thus make this the asylum of the oppressed of the whole earth.

We have this great mission to perform, and it can only be performed by adhering faithfully to that principle of self-government on which our institutions were all established. I repeat that the principle is the right of each state, each territory, to decide this slavery question for itself, to have slavery or not, as it chooses, and it does not become Mr. Lincoln, or anybody else, to tell the people of Kentucky that they have no conscience, that they are living in a state of iniquity, and that they are cherishing an institution to their bosoms in violation of the law of God. Better for him to adopt the doctrine of "judge not lest ye shall be judged." ["Good" and applause.] *Let him perform his own duty at home, and he will have a better fate in the future. I think there are objects of charity enough in the free states to excite the sympathies and open the pockets of all the benevolence we have amongst us, without going abroad in search of negroes, of whose condition we know nothing. We have enough objects of charity at home, and it is our duty to take care of our own poor, and our own suffering, and make them comfortable and happy, before we go abroad to intermeddle with other people's business.*

Lincoln: *My friends: I wish to return to Judge Douglas my profound thanks for his public annunciation here today, to be put on record, that his system of policy in regard to the institution of slavery* contemplates that it shall last forever. [Great cheers, and cries of "Hit him again."] *We are getting a little nearer the true issue of this controversy, and I am profoundly grateful for this one sentence. Judge Douglas asks you why cannot the institution of slavery, or rather, why cannot the nation, part slave and part free, continue as our fathers made it* forever? *In the first place, I insist that our fathers did not make this nation half slave and half free, or part slave and part free.* [Applause.] *I insist that they found the institution of slavery existing here. They did not make it so, but they left it so because they knew of no way to get rid of it at that time. When Judge Douglas undertakes to say that, as a matter of choice, the fathers of the government made this nation part slave and part free,* he assumes what is, historically, a falsehood. [Applause.] *More than that, when the fathers of the government cut off the source of slavery by the abolition of the slave trade, and adopted a system of restricting it from the new territories where it had not existed, I maintain that they placed it where they understood, and all sensible men understood, it was in the course of ultimate extinction. And when Judge Douglas asks me why it cannot continue as our fathers made it, I ask him why he and his friends could not let it remain as our fathers made it?* [Cheers.]

Judge Douglas could not let it stand upon the basis which our fathers placed it, but removed it and put it upon the cotton-gin basis. [Laughter, applause.] *It is a question, therefore, for him and his friends to answer—why they could not let it remain where the fathers of the government originally placed it?* [Cheers.]

CHAPTER 7

Seventh Debate, Alton, Illinois, October 15, 1858

The seventh and final debate took place just two days after the contest in Quincy. The setting was another Mississippi River town, this time Alton, Illinois, located more than a hundred miles downriver from Quincy and twenty miles upriver from St. Louis, Missouri. Alton had achieved a certain notoriety as the place where Elijah Lovejoy had been murdered for publishing his abolition broadsides, and the city was not much friendlier to the antislavery cause twenty years later. For the first time, Lincoln's wife, Mary, and their fifteen-year-old son, Robert, made the trip from Springfield to see Lincoln take on Mary's former suitor, the Little Giant. From a partisan perspective, both men had a good day. Both took a retrospective view, walking the audience through the whole of the contest, recurring to various moments in earlier debates. And both men did their best work tying their respective positions to America's first principles. For the first time Lincoln situated the battle to defeat the Slave Power as part of a larger "eternal struggle between . . . two principles—right and wrong—throughout the world. They are the two principles that have stood face to face from the beginning of time; and will ever continue to struggle. The one is the common right of humanity and the other the divine right of kings. It is the same principle in whatever shape it develops itself. It is the same spirit that says, 'You work and toil and earn bread, and I'll eat it.'" Douglas too rose to the moment, claiming that in telling the territories what they could and could not do without asking them, Lincoln was acting exactly like King George III. The men had saved their best performance for last; the rest would be in the hands of the voters.

Douglas: *Ladies and gentlemen: It is now nearly four months since the canvass between Mr. Lincoln and myself commenced. On the 16th of June the Republican convention assembled at Springfield and nominated Mr. Lincoln as their candidate for the U.S. Senate, and he, on that occasion, delivered a speech in which he laid down what he understood to be the Republican creed and the platform on which he proposed to stand during the contest.*

The principal points in that speech of Mr. Lincoln's were: First, that this government could not endure permanently divided into free and slave States, as our fathers made it; that they must all become free or all become slave; all become one thing or all become the other, otherwise this Union could not continue to exist. I give you his opinions almost in the identical language he used. His second proposition was a crusade against the Supreme Court of the United States because of the Dred Scott decision, urging as an especial reason for his opposition to that decision that it deprived the negroes of the rights and benefits of that clause in the Constitution of the United States which guaranties to the citizens of each state all the rights, privileges, and immunities of the citizens of the several states.

On the 10th of July I returned home, and delivered a speech to the people of Chicago, in which I announced it to be my purpose to appeal to the people of Illinois to sustain the course I had pursued in Congress. In that speech I joined issue with Mr. Lincoln on the points which he had presented. Thus there was an issue clear and distinct made up between us on these two propositions laid down in the speech of Mr. Lincoln at Springfield, and controverted by me in my reply to him at Chicago. On the next day the 11th of July Mr. Lincoln replied to me at Chicago, explaining at some length, and re-affirming the positions which he had taken in his Springfield speech. In that Chicago speech, he even went further than he had before and uttered sentiments in regard to the negro being on an equality with the white man. ["That's so."] He adopted in support of this position the argument which Lovejoy and Codding and other abolition lecturers had made familiar in the northern and central portions of the state, to wit: that the Declaration of Independence having declared all men free and equal, by Divine law also, that negro equality was an inalienable right, of which they could not be deprived.

The issue thus being made up between Mr. Lincoln and myself on three points, we went before the people of the state. During the following seven weeks, I took up Mr. Lincoln's three propositions in my several speeches, analyzed them, and pointed out what I believed to be the radical errors contained in them. First, in regard to his doctrine that this Government was in violation of the law of God which says that a house divided against itself cannot stand, I repudiated it as a slander upon the immortal framers of our Constitution. [Applause.] I then said, have often repeated, and now again assert, that in my opinion our government can endure forever, ["Good"] divided into free and slave States as our fathers made it, each state having the right to prohibit, abolish, or sustain slavery, just as it pleases. ["Good," "right," and cheers.]

If the people of Kansas want a slave State, they have a right to have it. If they wanted the Lecompton Constitution, they had a right to have it. I was opposed to that constitution because I did not believe that it was the act and deed of the people, but on the contrary, the act of a small, pitiful minority acting in the name of the majority. When at last it was determined to send *that constitution back to the people, and accordingly, in August last, the question of admission under it was submitted to a popular vote, the citizens rejected it by nearly ten to one, thus showing conclusively that I was right when I said that the Lecompton Constitution was not the act and deed of the people of Kansas and did not embody their will. [Cheers.]*

Most of the men who denounced my course on the Lecompton question, objected to it not because I was not right, but because they thought it expedient at that time, for the sake of keeping the party together, to do wrong. [Cheers.] I never knew the Democratic party to violate any one of its principles, out of policy or expediency, that it did not pay the debt with sorrow. There is no safety or success for our party unless we always do right, and trust the consequences to God and the people. I chose not to depart from principle for the sake of expediency in the Lecompton question, and I never intend to do it on that or any other question. ["Good."]

And now this warfare is made on me because I would not surrender my connections of duty, because I would not abandon my constituency, and receive the orders of the executive authorities how I should vote in the Senate of the United States. [Cheers.] I hold that an attempt to control the Senate on the part of the Executive is subversive of the principles of our Constitution. The Executive department is independent of the Senate, and the Senate is independent of the President. In matters of legislation the President has a veto on the action of the Senate, and in appointments and treaties the Senate has a veto on the President. He has no more right to tell me how I shall vote on his appointments than I have to tell him whether he shall veto or approve a bill that the Senate has passed. Whenever you recognize the right of the Executive to say to a Senator, "Do this, or I will take off the heads of your friends," you convert this government from a republic into a despotism.

Lincoln: *Ladies and gentlemen:*

A Voice: "There are no ladies here."

Lincoln: *You are mistaken about that. There is a fine chance of them back here [gesturing to wife; laughter.]*

This is the seventh time Judge Douglas and myself have met in these joint discussions, and he has been gradually improving in regard to his war with the administration. [Laughter, "That's so."] At Quincy, day before yesterday, he was a little more severe upon the administration than I had heard him upon any former occasion, and I took pains to compliment him for it. I then told him to give it to them with all the power he had, and as some of them were present, I told them I would be very much obliged if they would give it to him in about the same way. [Uproarious laughter and cheers.] I take it he has now vastly improved upon the attack he made then upon the administration. I flatter myself he has really taken my advice on this subject. All I can say now is to re-commend to him and to them what I then commended—to prosecute

*the war against one another in the most vigorous manner. I say to them again,
"Go it, husband! Go it, bear!"* [Great laughter.]

Douglas: *Mr. Lincoln['s] first criticism upon me is the expression of his hope
that the war of the Administration will be prosecuted against me and the
Democratic party of this state with vigor. He wants that war prosecuted with
vigor, I have no doubt of it. His hopes of success, and the hopes of his party
depend solely upon it. [This said] there is something really refreshing in the
thought that Mr. Lincoln is in favor of prosecuting one war vigorously. [Roars
of laughter.] It is the first war I ever knew him to be in favor of prosecuting.
[Renewed laughter, applause.] It is the first war that I ever knew him to believe to be just or constitutional. [Laughter and cheers.] When the Mexican
War was being waged, and the American army was surrounded by the enemy
in Mexico, he thought that war was unconstitutional, unnecessary, and unjust.
["That's so," "you've got him," "he voted against it," &c.] He thought it was
not commenced on the right spot. [Laughter.]*

*The Abolition party really think that under the Declaration of Independence
the negro is equal to the white man, and that negro equality is an inalienable
right conferred by the Almighty, and hence, that all human laws in violation of
it are null and void. With such men it is no use for me to argue. I hold that the
signers of the Declaration of Independence had no reference to negroes at all
when they declared all men to be created equal. They did not mean negro, nor
the savage Indians, nor the Fejee Islanders, nor any other barbarous race.
They were speaking of white men. ["It's so," "it's so," and cheers.] They alluded to men of European birth and European descent, to white men and to
none others, when they declared that doctrine. ["That's the truth."]*

Lincoln: *I have heard the Judge state two or three times what he has stated
today—that I had in a very especial manner complained that the Supreme
Court in the Dred Scott case had decided that a negro could never be a citizen
of the United States. I have omitted by some accident heretofore to analyze
this statement, and it is required of me to notice it now. In point of fact it is
untrue. I never have complained especially of the Dred Scott decision because
it held that a negro could not be a citizen, and the Judge is always wrong when
he says I ever did so complain of it.*

*Let me tell this audience what is true in regard to that matter. I spoke of the
Dred Scott decision in my Springfield speech, and I was then endeavoring to
prove that the Dred Scott decision was a portion of a system or scheme to
make slavery national in this country. I pointed out what things had been decided by the court. I mentioned as a fact that they had decided that a negro
could not be a citizen, that they had done so, as I supposed, to deprive the
negro, under all circumstances, of the remotest possibility of ever becoming a
citizen and claiming the rights of a citizen of the United States under a certain
clause of the Constitution. I stated that without making any complaint of it at
all. I then went on and stated the other points decided in the case, as evidence*

tending to prove a combination and conspiracy to make the institution of slavery national. In that connection and in that way I mentioned the decision on the point that a negro could not be a citizen, and in no other connection. Out of this, Judge Douglas builds up his beautiful fabrication of my purpose to introduce a perfect, social, and political equality between the white and black races.

I have stated upon former occasions, and I may as well state again, what I understand to be the real issue in this controversy between Judge Douglas and myself. On the point of my wanting to make war between the free and the slave states, there has been no issue between us. So, too, when he assumes that I am in favor of introducing a perfect social and political equality between the white and black races. These are false issues upon which Judge Douglas has tried to force the controversy. The real issue, the one pressing upon every mind, is the sentiment on the part of one class that looks upon the institution of slavery as a wrong, and of another class that does not look upon it as a wrong.

Has any thing ever threatened the existence of this Union save and except this very institution of slavery? What is it that we hold most dear amongst us? Our own liberty and prosperity. What has ever threatened our liberty and prosperity save and except this institution of slavery? If this is true, how do you propose to improve the condition of things? By enlarging slavery, by spreading it out and making it bigger? You may have a wen or cancer upon your person and not be able to cut it out lest you bleed to death. But surely it is no way to cure it, to engraft it and spread it over your whole body. That is no proper way of treating what you regard a wrong. You see this peaceful way of dealing with it as a wrong, restricting the spread of it, and not allowing it to go into new countries where it has not already existed. That is the peaceful way, the old-fashioned way, the way in which the fathers themselves set us the example.

[Douglas] says that upon the score of equality, slaves should be allowed to go in a new territory like other property. This is strictly logical if there is no difference between it and other property. If it and other property are equal, his argument is entirely logical. But if you insist that one is wrong and the other right, there is no use to institute a comparison between right and wrong. You may turn over every thing in the Democratic policy from beginning to end, whether in the shape it takes on the statute book, in the shape it takes in the Dred Scott decision, in the shape it takes in conversation, or the shape it takes in short maxim-like arguments. It every where carefully excludes the idea that there is any thing wrong in it.

That is the real issue. That is the issue that will continue in this country when these poor tongues of Judge Douglas and myself shall be silent. It is the eternal struggle between these two principles, right and wrong, throughout the world. They are the two principles that have stood face to face from the beginning of time, and will ever continue to struggle. The one is the common

right of humanity, and the other the divine right of kings. It is the same princi-
ple in whatever shape it develops itself. It is the same old serpent that says,
"You work and toil and earn bread, and I'll eat it." [Applause.] No matter in
what shape it comes, whether from the mouth of a king who seeks to bestride
the people of his own nation and live by the fruit of their labor, or from one
race of men as an apology for enslaving another race, it is the same tyrannical
principle.

Douglas: *Mr. Lincoln told you that the slavery question was the only thing*
that ever disturbed the peace and harmony of the Union. Did not nullification
once raise its head and disturb the peace of this Union in 1832? Was that the
slavery question, Mr. Lincoln? Did not disunion raise its monster head during
the last war with Great Britain? Was that the slavery question, Mr. Lincoln?
The peace of this country has been disturbed three times, once during the war
with Great Britain, once on the tariff question, and once on the slavery ques-
tion. ["Three cheers for Douglas."] His argument, therefore, that slavery is
the only question that has ever created dissension in the Union falls to the
ground.

Mr. Lincoln tries to avoid the main issue by attacking the truth of my propo-
sition, that our fathers made this Government divided into free and slave
states, recognizing the right of each to decide all its local questions for itself.
Did they not thus make it? But Mr. Lincoln says that when our fathers made
this government they did not look forward to the state of things now existing,
and therefore he thinks the doctrine was wrong. And he [finds] quotes to prove
that our fathers then thought that probably slavery would be abolished by
each state acting for itself before this time. Suppose they did. Suppose they did
not foresee what has occurred. Does that change the principles of our govern-
ment? They did not probably foresee the telegraph that transmits intelligence
by lightning, nor did they foresee the railroads that now form the bonds of
union between the different states, or the thousand mechanical inventions
that have elevated mankind. But do these things change the principles of the
government? Our fathers, I say, made this Government on the principle of
the right of each State to do as it pleases in its own domestic affairs, subject to
the Constitution, and allowed the people of each to apply to every new change
of circumstances such remedy as they may see fit to improve their condition.
This right they have for all time to come. [Cheers.]

Mr. Lincoln went on to tell you that he does not at all desire to interfere
with slavery in the States where it exists, nor does his party. I expected him to
say that down here. [Laughter.] Let me ask him then how he expects to put
slavery in the course of ultimate extinction everywhere, if he does not intend
to interfere with it in the states where it exists? His idea is that he will prohibit
slavery in all the territories and thus force them all to become free states,
surrounding the slave states with a cordon of free states and hemming them
in, keeping the slaves confined to their present limits, whilst they go on

multiplying until the soil on which they live will no longer feed them, and he will thus be able to put slavery in a course of ultimate extinction by starvation. [Cheers.] He will extinguish slavery in the Southern States as the French general exterminated the Algerines when he smoked them out. He is going to extinguish slavery by surrounding the slave States, hemming in the slaves and starving them out of existence as you smoke a fox out of his hole. He intends to do that in the name of humanity and Christianity, in order that we may get rid of the terrible crime and sin entailed upon our fathers of holding slaves. [Laughter and cheers.] Mr. Lincoln marks out that line of policy, and appeals to the moral sense of justice and to the Christian feeling of the community to sustain him. He says that any man who holds to the contrary doctrine is in the position of the king who claimed to govern by divine right. Let us examine for a moment and see what principle it was that overthrew the divine right of George the Third to govern us. Did not these colonies rebel because the British parliament had no right to pass laws concerning our property and domestic and private institutions without our consent? We demanded that the British Government should not pass such laws unless they gave us representation in the body passing them, and this the British government insisting on doing. We went to war on the principle that the home government should not control and govern distant colonies without giving them a representation. Now, Mr. Lincoln proposes to govern the territories without giving them a representation, and calls on Congress to pass laws controlling their property and domestic concerns without their consent and against their will. Thus, he asserts for his party the identical principle asserted by George III and the Tories of the Revolution. [Cheers.]

My friends, if, as I have said before, we will only live up to this great fundamental principle, there will be peace between the North and the South.

✳

Epilogue

The term "October Surprise" became a standard of the American political lexicon only in 1972 when, twelve days before the presidential election, Nixon's national security advisor, Henry Kissinger, announced at a White House press briefing that "peace [was] at hand" in Vietnam. Nixon probably did not need this last-minute goosing of the polls to defeat Democrat George McGovern, but ever since campaigns have tended to hold something in reserve, whether achievement or scandal, until it can be deployed to maximum effect just before election day.

Precedent setting in so many ways, the Lincoln–Douglas debates featured this maneuver as well. On October 19, four days after the final debate in Alton and less than three weeks before the polls were to open, Theophilus Dickey, a Douglas partisan and Old Line Whig, pulled from his pocket a letter that had been written before the campaign ever commenced endorsing Douglas for Senator. The letter had been written by John Jordan Crittenden, arguably the greatest living Whig, inheritor of Henry Clay's Kentucky Senate seat and with it the mantle of "Great Pacificator." (It was also estimated that Crittenden controlled as many as 20,000 votes in Illinois.)

Crittenden's endorsement (and gerrymandered districts) likely determined Lincoln's fate. On election day, Lincoln won the popular vote by 3,402 votes, giving him a margin of 50.6%. But in an age when Senators were chosen not by the people but by the state houses, the district races were the ones that mattered. There Democrats carried 40 seats to the Republicans' 35. Combined with incumbents, this left the balance in the house at Republicans 46, Democrats 54. The Illinois House made it official on January 5, 1859, when it returned Stephen Arnold Douglas to the U.S. Senate chamber.

The day after the election, Lincoln was deluged with condolences. Some of his operatives were raw and despondent. "The lever of Judge Dickey's influence has been felt," lamented Lincoln's close associate, David Davis. "[The way] he drew [that] letter out of Mr. Crittenden . . . was perfectly outrageous." "I assume that, having the power, the [Douglasites] will [now] so district the State that we will be sold

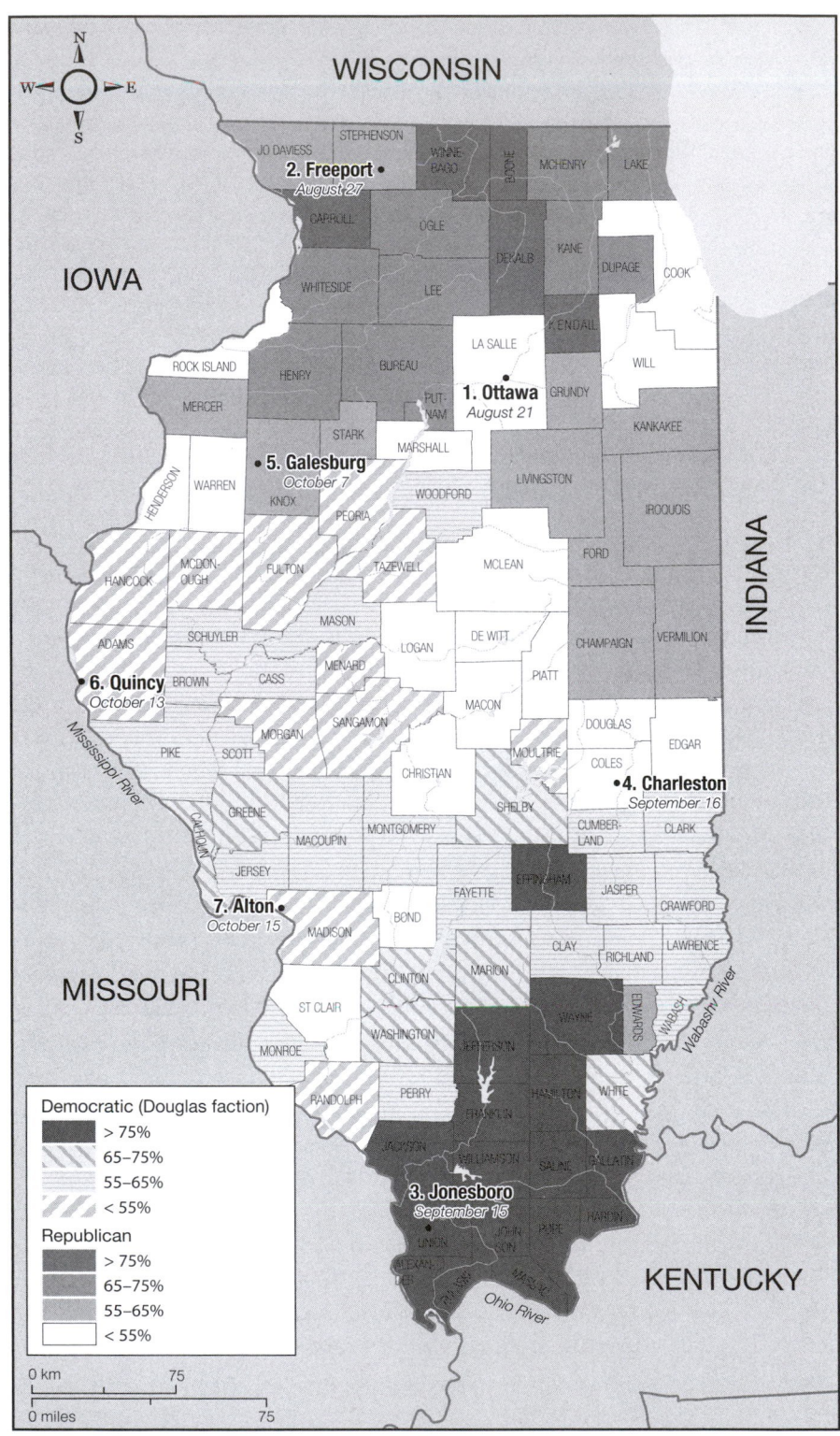

Election Results, Illinois, 1858

permanently," wrote Illinois state senator Norman Judd. Other Lincoln partisans took a more far-sighted view. "You have planted the seed that will germinate & ripen in to glorious fruit," two lawyers wrote Lincoln from Bloomington. "You have made a national reputation that I would much rather have this day than that of S. A. Douglas." Fayette County judge Henry Bromwell was even more prescient. "The way seems paved for the presidential victory of 1860," he wrote Lincoln. "[You need only] a wider field to meet our enemies where they cannot skulk behind gerymandered . . . lines." Lincoln, typically, was both more stoic about his loss and humble about his prospects. "For the future my view is that the fight must go on," he said, and "in that day I shall fight in the ranks [and] be in no one's way for any of the places."[18]

The Election of 1860 would pit Lincoln and Douglas against each other again, although they would never again share a stage until inauguration day, when Douglas magnanimously agreed to hold Lincoln's hat while he took the presidential oath of office. Douglas is rarely given enough credit for, however inadvertently and regretfully, bringing Lincoln's inauguration about. If nothing else, he had been the critical whetstone in sharpening Lincoln's mind and oratory for a run at the presidency. Lincoln's first debate was arguably his weakest. His last was arguably his strongest. Douglas may not have evolved as much during the course of the debates, but Lincoln could not have evolved at all without him. Indeed, Lincoln's entire problem was that Douglas was occupying the very piece of political real estate he needed for himself, the high ground of American partisan warfare, the mantle of the Founding Fathers, and the appearance as the true conservative. As long as Douglas could claim that ground too, Lincoln's ideas had no more legitimacy than Douglas's. What Lincoln needed to do, and what he finally did, was seize that high ground in such a way as to put it forever beyond Douglas's grasp.

This is what Lincoln accomplished at Cooper Union in February 1860, in a speech that ought to be regarded as the eighth and final Lincoln–Douglas debate—the coda and codicil to a dialogue that began in Ottawa and the culmination of Lincoln's entire Douglas-inspired evolution. To be sure, the two men did not, in this "eighth" encounter, debate each other on the same stage as they had in Illinois. But by 1860 they were arguably always in each other's minds, and they battled now not on any one stage but in the national press. In September 1859, as his own presidential bid began to heat up, Douglas gave a speech at Columbus, Ohio, not substantially different from the ones he had given in Illinois in 1858. In his peroration he said, "Our fathers, when they framed this Government under which we live, understood this question [meaning the slavery question] just as well, and even better, than we do now." He meant what he had always said—the Founders had compromised; they had created a country where slavery was legal; they had believed that states could decide the slavery question for themselves, and we should leave it at that. Lincoln had taken many swings at this argument during the 1858 debates, and each swing had been more effective than the last, but never did he notch so careful an arrow to kill it as he did at Cooper Union.

The first two words of Lincoln's speech are "the facts," which is a fair introduction to the parade of figures that follows. Lincoln's law partner said that he had never seen Lincoln work so hard or do so much research as he did for his Cooper Union talk. But Lincoln was determined not to deliver a stem-winder but a history lesson, and it proved one of the greatest history lessons in the history of American politics.

The Cooper Union Address is also notable for its final line. The speech had not begun auspiciously. Lincoln had shuffled his papers; his voice, face, and general lankiness had made their usual, unfavorable first impression. But by the end of the speech, witnesses said that Lincoln had the audience in the palm of his hand. "My face [was] glowing . . . my frame all aquiver," said one member of the crowd. When "a friend, with his eyes aglow, asked me what I thought of Abe Lincoln, the rail-splitter, I said 'He's the greatest man since St. Paul!'" When Lincoln rose to his peroration, then, telling the crowd, "Let us have faith that RIGHT MAKES MIGHT, and in that faith, let us, to the end, dare to do our duty," the audience was on its feet, ready to be dared to do anything. Why then did Lincoln append "as we understand it" to that final triumphal line? Why did he dampen the mood by raising the specter that men often don't know their own duty aright? It is worth noting that he marred his Second Inaugural Address in exactly the same way: "With malice toward none, with charity for all, with firmness in the right as God gives us to see the right, let us strive on to finish the work we are in." Even in his moment of triumph, Lincoln never forgot, and never let his audience forget, that the presumption of rightness is the gateway to self-righteousness, a moral and political sin leading to bad thinking, bad decisions, and bad policy.

DOUGLAS AT COLUMBUS, OHIO, SEPTEMBER 7, 1859

Fellow-Citizens of Ohio: In compliance with the invitation of your State Central Committee, I appear before you to-day for the purpose of discussing some of those great leading topics which now agitate the public mind of this country. I maintain any political creed to be unsound which cannot be avowed in Chicago the same as in New-Orleans. If the Democratic creed cannot be avowed and practiced in Ohio the same as in Kentucky, in the North as well as in the South, there must be something radically wrong. So long as we live under a common Constitution, which is the supreme law of the entire public, our political creed should be as broad as the Republic and as universal as that Constitution. I wish to invite your attention to-day to those great principles which underlie the Democratic Creed, and draw the dividing line between the Democracy and all the other political parties in this country upon this vexed question of Slavery. The Democratic Party hold that it is the right of the people of every State, of every Territory and every political community within this Confederacy to decide that question to suit themselves. We not only apply that principle to the question of Slavery, but we extend it to all the local and domestic institutions of all the States and all the Territories of the Union. On the other hand, we are told by the leaders of the Republican Party that there is an irrepressible conflict between Freedom and Slavery, free labor and slave labor, Free States and Slave States, and that it is their intention to continue to excite, agitate and divide the country until Slavery shall be abolished or established throughout the country. In other words, the Republican Party hold that there must be uniformity in the local institutions of all the States and Territories of the Union. Mr. Seward, in his Rochester speech, says that it is an irrepressible conflict between enduring force, that must last until uniformity is established. Mr. Lincoln, in the Illinois canvass of last year, compared it to a house divided against itself which could not stand, and said that this Union could not permanently endure divided into Free and Slave States, as our fathers made it.

Read the history of the Colonies up to the time of the Revolution, and you will find upon the statute books of every one of the thirteen, enactments regulating and controlling this Slavery question. Assembled for the first time, in 1774, they for their first act adopted a Bill of Rights for the Colonies. Look into that Bill of Rights, and you will find the great foundation principles upon which all of our institutions have been based since in that Bill of Rights. The Colonies first declared that they are willing to grant to Great Britain the right to regulate commerce and decide all their questions of a general character, but they said that they claimed for themselves the free and exclusive power of legislation in their provincial Legislatures upon all subjects of internal policy. There is the principle, distinctly asserted, for which they went to war. It was the principle that every colony has a right to decide for itself, in its own Legislature, all questions of taxation and internal policy. It will be seen, therefore, that the Tories of the Revolution held at that day that the Imperial Parliament had a right to govern the Territories as it pleased. The Colonies, on the other hand, denied that pretension of the Tories, and said that they as Colonies had the exclusive right to decide all questions of Territorial policy, Slavery included, to suit themselves. The Declaration of Independence was put forth, and all the battles of the Revolution were fought in vindication of that great principle. Our fathers did not at first desire independence—the protested that they did not wish to separate from Great Britain; but what they contended for was the right of local self-government in their internal affaires, without the interference of Parliament, and if they could not obtain that right under the British Government, they would declare their independence and fight for the right. They did fight the battle out nobly, for seven long years. The carried in triumph the flag of local self-government for the Colonies, until at last Great Britain recognized their independence, and the war ceased.

After the independence was established, the different States ceded to the Federal Government the land which they held in the western country to the

*north of the Ohio River. This country, where we are now assembled, belonged
to the State of Virginia, and she ceded it to the Government—first for the
common benefit of the Union, on condition that it should be formed into
States and admitted into the Union on an equal footing with the original
States. That deed of cession was accepted on the 1st day of March, 1784, and
on the same day Thos. Jefferson, the author of the Declaration of Independence, reported his plan for the government of the new Territories or new
States west of the Ohio River. By that plan the Territories were recognized as
States, the people having the right to decide all international questions to suit
themselves. It is true that Mr. Jefferson proposed to obtain their consent to a
proposition prohibiting Slavery—not that the present Government has the
right or power—but he asked for their consent to such a compact, and Congress struck out the clause and passed the plan of Mr. Jefferson recognizing
these Territories as States and the right of the people inhabiting them to
decide the Slavery question to suit themselves, without the interference of
Congress or any other State or power on earth.*

*Thus you find that up to the time the Constitution was adopted this great
principle of local self-government was maintained in the government of the
new Territories, or new States as they were then called.*

*Now let me ask you, is it reasonable to suppose, after our fathers had fought
the battles of the Revolution in behalf of the right of each Colony to govern
itself in respect to its local and domestic concerns, that then they conferred
upon Congress the arbitrary sovereign power which they had refused to the
British Parliament? [Cries of "Never."] Our fathers, previous to the Revolution,
declared that it was the inalienable birthright of Englishmen, when forming
political communities, to govern themselves in their internal polity. Now if that
was the birthright of Englishmen before the Revolution, did it not become the
birthright of all Americans after the Revolution? I only claim for the people of
the Territories those same rights for which our fathers fought for the American
Colonies. Remember the Revolution was not fought for the rights of sovereign
States. Our fathers were contending for the rights of Colonies, of Provinces,
of dependent Territories, when they asserted this inalienable right of local
self-government, and we are asserting now, in behalf of the people of the
American Territories, the same great inalienable right. Why should it not be
granted? The Republicans tell us that they are willing to grant this right of
self-government in the Territories in all cases excepting the negro. They do not
deny that the people of the Territories are capable of making all laws to regulate the relations of husband and wife, parent and child, and guardian and
ward, or all laws affecting white men; but, there is something so sacred in the
rights of the negro that they will not trust them to the same legislature that
controls yours and mine. [Laughter and cheers.] If we will only apply the great
principle of non-intervention by Congress, and self-government in the Territories, leaving the people to do as they please, there will be peace and harmony*

between all sections of the Union. What interest have you in Ohio in the question of Slavery in South Carolina? You say that you do not think that Slavery is necessary or beneficial. That may be true, but your opinion might be different if your property was all invested in a nice plantation in South Carolina, where the white man cannot live and cultivate the soil. In Ohio it is a question only between the white man and the negro. [Laughter.] But if you go further South you will find that it is a question between the negro and the crocodile. [Renewed laughter.]

The question then may be a very different one under different climates. Our fathers, when they framed this Government under which we live, understood this question just as well, and even better, than we do now. They knew when they made this Republic that a country so broad as ours with such a variety of climate, soil and productions, must have a variety of interests, requiring different laws adapted to each locality.

LINCOLN AT COOPER UNION, NEW YORK, FEBRUARY 27, 1860

Mr. President and fellow citizens of New York:—

The facts with which I shall deal this evening are mainly old and familiar; nor is there anything new in the general use I shall make of them. If there shall be any novelty, it will be in the mode of presenting the facts, and the inferences and observations following that presentation.

In his speech last autumn, at Columbus, Ohio, as reported in "The New-York Times," Senator Douglas said:

"Our fathers, when they framed the Government under which we live, understood this question just as well, and even better, than we do now."

I fully indorse this, and I adopt it as a text for this discourse. I so adopt it because it furnishes a precise and an agreed starting point for a discussion between Republicans and that wing of the Democracy headed by Senator Douglas. It simply leaves the inquiry: "What was the understanding those fathers had of the question mentioned?"

What is the frame of government under which we live?

The answer must be: "The Constitution of the United States." That Constitution consists of the original, framed in 1787 (and under which the present government first went into operation), and twelve subsequently framed amendments, the first ten of which were framed in 1789.

Who were our fathers that framed the Constitution? I suppose the "thirty-nine" who signed the original instrument may be fairly called our fathers who framed that part of the present Government. It is almost exactly true to say they framed it, and it is altogether true to say they fairly represented the opinion and sentiment of the whole nation at that time. Their names, being familiar to nearly all, and accessible to quite all, need not now be repeated.

I take these "thirty-nine," for the present, as being "our fathers who framed the Government under which we live."

What is the question which, according to the text, those fathers understood "just as well, and even better than we do now?"

It is this: Does the proper division of local from federal authority, or anything in the Constitution, forbid our Federal Government to control as to slavery in our Federal Territories?

Upon this, Senator Douglas holds the affirmative, and Republicans the negative. This affirmation and denial form an issue; and this issue—this question—is precisely what the text declares our fathers understood "better than we."

Let us now inquire whether the "thirty-nine," or any of them, ever acted upon this question; and if they did, how they acted upon it—how they expressed that better understanding?

In 1784, three years before the Constitution—the United States then owning the Northwestern Territory, and no other, the Congress of the Confederation had before them the question of prohibiting slavery in that Territory; and four of the "thirty-nine" who afterward framed the Constitution, were in that Congress, and voted on that question. Of these, Roger Sherman, Thomas Mifflin, and Hugh Williamson voted for the prohibition, thus showing that, in their understanding, no line dividing local from federal authority, nor anything else, properly forbade the Federal Government to control as to slavery in federal territory.

In 1787, still before the Constitution, but while the Convention was in session framing it, and while the Northwestern Territory still was the only territory owned by the United States, the same question of prohibiting slavery in the territory again came before the Congress of the Confederation; and two more of the "thirty-nine" who afterward signed the Constitution, were in that Congress, and voted on the question. They were William Blount and William Few; and they both voted for the prohibition—thus showing that, in their understanding, no line dividing local from federal authority, nor anything else, properly forbids the Federal Government to control as to slavery in Federal territory.

In 1789, by the first Congress which sat under the Constitution, an act was passed to enforce the Ordinance of '87, including the prohibition of slavery in the Northwestern Territory. The bill for this act was reported by one of the "thirty-nine," Thomas Fitzsimmons, then a member of the House of Representatives from Pennsylvania. It went through all its stages without a word of opposition, and finally passed both branches without yeas and nays, which is equivalent to a unanimous passage. In this Congress there were sixteen of the thirty-nine fathers who framed the original Constitution. This shows that, in their understanding, no line dividing local from federal authority, nor anything in the Constitution, properly forbade Congress to prohibit slavery in the federal territory.

Again, George Washington, another of the "thirty-nine," was then President of the United States, and, as such approved and signed the bill; thus completing its validity as a law, and thus showing that, in his understanding, no line dividing local from federal authority, nor anything in the Constitution, forbade the Federal Government, to control as to slavery in federal territory.

No great while after the adoption of the original Constitution, North Carolina ceded to the Federal Government the country now constituting the State of Tennessee; and a few years later Georgia ceded that which now constitutes the States of Mississippi and Alabama. In both deeds of cession it was made a condition by the ceding States that the Federal Government should not prohibit slavery in the ceded territory. This act passed both branches of Congress without yeas and nays. In that Congress were three of the "thirty-nine" who framed the original Constitution. They were John Langdon, George Read and Abraham Baldwin.

In 1803, the Federal Government purchased the Louisiana country from a foreign nation. In 1804, Congress gave a territorial organization to that part of it which now constitutes the State of Louisiana. Congress did not, in the Territorial Act, prohibit slavery; but [provided]:

First. That no slave should be imported into the territory from foreign parts.

Second. That no slave should be carried into it who had been imported into the United States since the first day of May, 1798.

Third. That no slave should be carried into it, except by the owner, and for his own use as a settler; the penalty in all the cases being a fine upon the violator of the law, and freedom to the slave.

This act also was passed without yeas and nays. In the Congress which passed it, there were two of the "thirty-nine."

In 1819–20, came and passed the Missouri question. Many votes were taken, by yeas and nays, in both branches of Congress, upon the various phases of the general question. Two of the "thirty-nine"—Rufus King and Charles Pinckney—were members of that Congress. Mr. King steadily voted for slavery prohibition and against all compromises, while Mr. Pinckney as steadily voted against slavery prohibition and against all compromises. By this, Mr. King showed that, in his understanding, no line dividing local from federal authority, nor anything in the Constitution, was violated by Congress prohibiting slavery in federal territory; while Mr. Pinckney, by his votes, showed that, in his understanding, there was some sufficient reason for opposing such prohibition in that case.

Here, then, we have twenty-three out of our thirty-nine fathers "who framed the government under which we live," who have, upon their official responsibility and their corporal oaths, acted [as if nothing] forbade the Federal Government to control as to slavery in the federal territories.

The remaining sixteen of the "thirty-nine," so far as I have discovered, have left no record of their understanding upon the direct question of federal control of slavery in the federal territories. But there is much reason to believe *that their understanding upon that question would not have appeared different from that of their twenty-three compeers, had it been manifested at all.*

And so assuming, I defy any man to show that any one of them ever, in his whole life, declared that, in his understanding, any proper division of local from federal authority, or any part of the Constitution, forbade the Federal Government to control as to slavery in the federal territories. I go a step further. I defy any one to show that any living man in the whole world ever did, prior to the beginning of the present century, (and I might almost say prior to the beginning of the last half of the present century,) declare that, in his understanding, any proper division of local from federal authority, or any part of the Constitution, forbade the Federal Government to control as to slavery in the federal territories. To those who now so declare, I give, not only "our fathers who framed the Government under which we live," but with them all other living men within the century in which it was framed, among whom to search, and they shall not be able to find the evidence of a single man agreeing with them.

[So] let all who believe that "our fathers, who framed the Government under which we live, understood this question just as well, and even better, than we do now," speak as they spoke, and act as they acted upon it. This is all Republicans ask—all Republicans desire—in relation to slavery. As those fathers marked it, so let it be again marked, as an evil not to be extended, but to be tolerated and protected only because of and so far as its actual presence among us makes that toleration and protection a necessity. Let all the guarantees those fathers gave it, be, not grudgingly, but fully and fairly, maintained. *For this Republicans contend, and with this, so far as I know or believe, they will be content.*

And now, if they would listen—as I suppose they will not—I would address a few words to the Southern people.

I would say to them:—You consider yourselves a reasonable and a just people; and I consider that in the general qualities of reason and justice you are not inferior to any other people. Still, when you speak of us Republicans, you do so only to denounce us as reptiles, or, at the best, as no better than outlaws. You will grant a hearing to pirates or murderers, but nothing like it to "Black Republicans."

You say we are sectional. We deny it. That makes an issue; and the burden of proof is upon you. You produce your proof; and what is it? Why, that our party has no existence in your section—gets no votes in your section. The fact is substantially true; but does it prove the issue? If it does, then in case we should, without change of principle, begin to get votes in your section, we should thereby cease to be sectional. You cannot escape this conclusion; and yet, are you willing to abide by it? If you are, you will probably soon find that we have ceased to be sectional, for we shall get votes in your section this very year. You will then begin to discover, as the truth plainly is, that your proof does not touch the issue. The fact that we get no votes in your section, is a fact of your making, and not of ours.

Some of you delight to flaunt in our faces the warning against sectional parties given by Washington in his Farewell Address. Less than eight years before Washington gave that warning, he had, as President of the United States, approved and signed an act of Congress, enforcing the prohibition of slavery in the Northwestern Territory, which act embodied the policy of the Government upon that subject up to and at the very moment he penned that warning; and about one year after he penned it, he wrote LaFayette that he considered that prohibition a wise measure, expressing in the same connection his hope that we should at some time have a confederacy of free States.

Bearing this in mind, and seeing that sectionalism has since arisen upon this same subject, is that warning a weapon in your hands against us, or in our hands against you? Could Washington himself speak, would he cast the blame of that sectionalism upon us, who sustain his policy, or upon you who repudiate it?

But you say you are conservative—eminently conservative—while we are revolutionary, destructive, or something of the sort. What is conservatism? Is it not adherence to the old and tried, against the new and untried? We stick to, contend for, the identical old policy on the point in controversy which was adopted by "our fathers who framed the Government under which we live;" while you with one accord reject, and scout, and spit upon that old policy, and insist upon substituting something new.

Again, you say we have made the slavery question more prominent than it formerly was. We deny it. We admit that it is more prominent, but we deny that we made it so. It was not we, but you, who discarded the old policy of the fathers.

You charge that we stir up insurrections among your slaves. We deny it; and what is your proof? Harper's Ferry! John Brown!! John Brown was no Republican; and you have failed to implicate a single Republican in his Harper's Ferry enterprise. If any member of our party is guilty in that matter, you know it or you do not know it. If you do know it, you are inexcusable for not designating the man and proving the fact. If you do not know it, you are inexcusable for asserting it, and especially for persisting in the assertion after you have tried and failed to make the proof. You need to be told that persisting in a charge which one does not know to be true, is simply malicious slander.

Some of you admit that no Republican designedly aided or encouraged the Harper's Ferry affair, but still insist that our doctrines and declarations necessarily lead to such results. We do not believe it. We know we hold to no doctrine, and make no declaration, which were not held to and made by "our fathers who framed the Government under which we live." True, we do, in common with "our fathers, who framed the Government under which we live," declare our belief that slavery is wrong; but the slaves do not hear us declare even this. For anything we say or do, the slaves would scarcely know there is a Republican party. I believe they would not, in fact, generally know it but for your misrepresentations of us, in their hearing. In your political contests among yourselves, each faction charges the other with sympathy with Black Republicanism; and then, to give point to the charge, defines Black Republicanism to simply be insurrection, blood and thunder among the slaves.

But you will break up the Union rather than submit to a denial of your Constitutional rights.

That has a somewhat reckless sound; but it would be palliated, if not fully justified, were we proposing, by the mere force of numbers, to deprive you of some right, plainly written down in the Constitution. But we are proposing no such thing.

When you make these declarations, you have a specific and well-understood allusion to an assumed Constitutional right of yours, to take slaves into the federal territories, and to hold them there as property. But no such right is specifically written in the Constitution. That instrument is literally silent about any such right. We, on the contrary, deny that such a right has any existence in the Constitution, even by implication.

Your purpose, then, plainly stated, is that you will destroy the Government, unless you be allowed to construe and enforce the Constitution as you please, on all points in dispute between you and us. You will rule or ruin in all events.

This, plainly stated, is your language. Perhaps you will say the Supreme Court has decided the disputed Constitutional question in your favor. Not quite so. The Court have decided the question for you in a sort of way. The Court have substantially said, it is your Constitutional right to take slaves into the federal territories, and to hold them there as property. When I say the decision was made in a sort of way, I mean it was made in a divided Court, by a bare majority of the Judges, and they not quite agreeing with one another in the reasons for making it; that it is so made as that its avowed supporters disagree with one another about its meaning, and that it was mainly based upon a mistaken statement of fact—the statement in the opinion that "the right of property in a slave is distinctly and expressly affirmed in the Constitution."

An inspection of the Constitution will show that the right of property in a slave is not "distinctly and expressly affirmed" in it. When this obvious mistake of the Judges shall be brought to their notice, is it not reasonable to expect that they will withdraw the mistaken statement, and reconsider the conclusion based upon it?

And then it is to be remembered that "our fathers, who framed the Government under which we live"—the men who made the Constitution—decided this same Constitutional question in our favor, long ago—decided it without division among themselves, when making the decision; without division among themselves about the meaning of it after it was made, and, so far as any evidence is left, without basing it upon any mistaken statement of facts.

Under all these circumstances, do you really feel yourselves justified to break up this Government unless such a court decision as yours is, shall be at once submitted to as a conclusive and final rule of political action? But you will not abide the election of a Republican president! In that supposed event, you say, you will destroy the Union; and then, you say, the great crime of having destroyed it will be upon us! That is cool. A highwayman holds a pistol to my ear, and mutters through his teeth, "Stand and deliver, or I shall kill you, and then you will be a murderer!"

To be sure, what the robber demanded of me—my money—was my own; and I had a clear right to keep it; but it was no more my own than my vote is my own; and the threat of death to me, to extort my money, and the threat of destruction to the Union, to extort my vote, can scarcely be distinguished in principle.

A few words now to Republicans. It is exceedingly desirable that all parts of this great Confederacy shall be at peace, and in harmony, one with another. Let us Republicans do our part to have it so. Even though much provoked, let us do nothing through passion and ill temper. Even though the southern people will not so much as listen to us, let us calmly consider their demands, and yield to them if, in our deliberate view of our duty, we possibly can. Judging by all they say and do, and by the subject and nature of their controversy with us, let us determine, if we can, what will satisfy them.

Will they be satisfied if the Territories be unconditionally surrendered to them? We know they will not. In all their present complaints against us, the Territories are scarcely mentioned. Invasions and insurrections are the rage now. Will it satisfy them, if, in the future, we have nothing to do with invasions and insurrections? We know it will not. We so know, because we know we never had anything to do with invasions and insurrections; and yet this total abstaining does not exempt us from the charge and the denunciation.

The question recurs, what will satisfy them? Simply this: We must not only let them alone, but we must somehow, convince them that we do let them alone. This, we know by experience, is no easy task. We have been so trying to convince them from the very beginning of our organization, but with no success. In all our platforms and speeches we have constantly protested our purpose to let them alone; but this has had no tendency to convince them. Alike unavailing to convince them, is the fact that they have never detected a man of us in any attempt to disturb them.

These natural, and apparently adequate means all failing, what will convince them? This, and this only: cease to call slavery wrong, and join them in calling it right. And this must be done thoroughly—done in acts as well as in words. Silence will not be tolerated—we must place ourselves avowedly with them. Senator Douglas' new sedition law must be enacted and enforced, suppressing all declarations that slavery is wrong, whether made in politics, in presses, in pulpits, or in private. We must arrest and return their fugitive slaves with greedy pleasure. We must pull down our Free State constitutions. The whole atmosphere must be disinfected from all taint of opposition to slavery, before they will cease to believe that all their troubles proceed from us.

I am quite aware they do not state their case precisely in this way. Most of them would probably say to us, "Let us alone, do nothing to us, and say what you please about slavery." But we do let them alone—have never disturbed them—so that, after all, it is what we say, which dissatisfies them. They will continue to accuse us of doing, until we cease saying.

Holding, as they do, that slavery is morally right, and socially elevating, they cannot cease to demand a full national recognition of it, as a legal right, and a social blessing. Nor can we justifiably withhold this, on any ground save our conviction that slavery is wrong. If slavery is right, all words, acts, laws, and constitutions against it, are themselves wrong, and should be silenced, and swept away. If it is right, we cannot justly object to its nationality—its universality; if it is wrong, they cannot justly insist upon its extension—its enlargement. All they ask, we could readily grant, if we thought slavery right; all we ask, they could as readily grant, if they thought it wrong. Their thinking it right, and our thinking it wrong, is the precise fact upon which depends the whole controversy. Thinking it right, as they do, they are not to blame for desiring its full recognition, as being right; but, thinking it wrong, as we do, can we yield to them? Can we cast our votes with their view, and against our own? In view of our moral, social, and political responsibilities, can we do this?

Wrong as we think slavery is, we can yet afford to let it alone where it is, because that much is due to the necessity arising from its actual presence in the nation; but can we, while our votes will prevent it, allow it to spread into the National Territories, and to overrun us here in these Free States? If our sense of duty forbids this, then let us stand by our duty, fearlessly and effectively. Let us be diverted by none of those sophistical contrivances wherewith we are so industriously plied and belabored—contrivances such as groping for some middle ground between the right and the wrong, vain as the search for a man who should be neither a living man nor a dead man—such as a policy of "don't care" on a question about which all true men do care—such as Union appeals beseeching true Union men to yield to Disunionists, reversing the divine rule, and calling, not the sinners, but the righteous to repentance— such as invocations to Washington, imploring men to unsay what Washington said, and undo what Washington did.

Neither let us be slandered from our duty by false accusations against us, nor frightened from it by menaces of destruction to the Government nor of dungeons to ourselves. LET US HAVE FAITH THAT RIGHT MAKES MIGHT, AND IN THAT FAITH, LET US, TO THE END, DARE TO DO OUR DUTY AS WE UNDERSTAND IT.

Lincoln Explains America to Itself

ON MARCH 4, 1861, Abraham Lincoln put his hand on the Bible and swore to "preserve, protect, and defend" a legal document that fully sanctioned slavery. The Constitution of the United States does not use the word slave, but it does refer euphemistically to "persons held to service or labor," and it does not scruple about enumerating them, providing for their protection as property, or requiring them to be delivered up as fugitives. Given this, the fact that Lincoln ultimately found a legal way, within the Constitution, to destroy something specifically sanctioned by it ought to fill us with awe.

And indeed it used to. For generations, Lincoln was "Father Abraham," the "Great Emancipator," and a second Moses leading the slaves out of Egypt. Now, quite rightly, scholars paint a more complicated portrait. Certainly Lincoln hated slavery with every fiber of his being. "If slavery is not wrong," he told a friend, "nothing is wrong." Slavery's existence, Lincoln said, had the *unique* power to make him "miserable." He could not "remember a time when [he] did not think the institution an evil," and by the 1850s he had learned to hate the sin of slavery enough to occasionally hate the sinner. "Whenever I hear anyone arguing [for] slavery," he said flatly, "I feel a strong impulse to see it tried on him personally."[19]

But it is harder to pin down Lincoln's attitudes toward race. He seemed mostly to duck the issue, which, as was his way, he tended to do with humor. The black man is not exactly my equal, Lincoln would say . . . at the very least because we are different colors. I do not want to marry a black woman, he would chuckle, but if Douglas does he can go on ahead, and if any other man wants to, he should do it, "if *she* can stand it." In these moments Lincoln is trying to make light of something he found incalculably heavy. We may never know whether Lincoln could imagine a future in which African Americans were equal in every aspect of American life. Probably he thought whites wouldn't let this happen; probably he was a white supremacist, at least in the sense that if someone had to win what he called "the race of life," he'd rather it be a white man.

But in this, as in most matters, I'm inclined to trust another Douglass—Frederick. "In all my interviews with Mr. Lincoln," noted the famed abolitionist, "I was impressed with his entire freedom from popular prejudice against the colored race. He was the first great man that I talked with . . . who in no single instance reminded me of the difference between himself and myself [on] the difference of color." In a later interview Douglass added, "There was [always a] feeling that I had with reference to [Lincoln], that while I felt in his presence I was in the presence of a very great man, as great as the greatest, I felt as though I could go and put my hand on him if I wanted to, to put my hand on his shoulder. Of course, I did not do it, but I felt that I could. I felt as though I was in the presence of a big brother, and that there was safety in his atmosphere." Douglass's choice of words is revealing. Human contact—touch—is where racial divisions finally and permanently dissolve. Racism brews like heavy weather; if Douglass felt "safety" in Lincoln's "atmosphere," he meant it.[20]

All of this is largely beside the point, however. Lincoln was not contending with racism. This is our battle, not his. Lincoln lived in a world where the Chief Justice of the Supreme Court, the highest legal authority in the country, had declared that a black man had *no rights* a white man was bound to respect—not a right to his labor, not a right to her body, not a right to their very being. A better sense of the depth of the era's racism can be gleaned from the writing of Mississippi's Henry Hughes, one of the Old South's lesser-known proslavery thinkers. According to Hughes, whites were uniquely fit for mental labor; blacks were uniquely fit for physical labor, and the state should compel them to it. "Let us . . . if expedient," he pronounced, "mark them like hogs and brand them like beeves; let us slit their nostrils . . . pinch in their bleeding ears . . . or, with hot and salted irons, fry on their brows and breasts lasting" badges of their race and status. Mulattoes, not fitting Hughes's clean labor categories, would have to be exterminated as the state's "ethnical duty." And "as to the pure blooded Indians," Hughes noted, "they will not be civilized, and therefore must, directly or indirectly, be benignly slaughtered." This was the world Lincoln contended against—a world with an enormously high tolerance for other people's pain, a world in which men were *legally* treated as things.[21]

That world is long gone (for the most part); slavery, although not dead, has been put to flight. But Lincoln remains relevant for another reason—because he, better than any other American, succeeded in explaining America to itself. From 1854 to 1860, Lincoln was focused on what the Constitution did and did not allow with respect to slavery in the territories. He did not, like William Lloyd Garrison, seek to "get around" the Constitution by literally burning it. And he did not, like William Seward, suggest that the Constitution should submit to a "Higher Power"—that of God's law. Lincoln was more conservative and less religious. He hoped to work within the Constitution to contain (and perhaps thereby eventually to strangle) slavery within a cordon of freedom.

But there was always a more radical strain to Lincoln's thinking that worked first at the back of his mind and gradually moved to the front: the sense that Garrison and Seward had been partly right. There *was* an authority higher than the Constitution, but it was not God and not the personal conscience; it was the Declaration of Independence.

Lincoln certainly mentioned the Declaration a great deal in his debates with Douglas—although it was often Douglas who brought it up. At Cooper Union, Lincoln was clear that the Constitution must answer to history and to the Founders' intent. But the first time he explicitly articulated the relationship he saw between the two documents was in a fragment that was probably written for his First Inaugural, although he left it undeployed amid his scraps. "Without the *Constitution* and the *Union*," Lincoln wrote, "we could not have attained the result [our success as a nation]; but even these are not the primary cause of our great prosperity. There is something back of these, entwining itself more closely about the human heart. That something, is the principle of "Liberty to all"—the principle that clears the *path* for all—gives *hope* to all—and, by consequence, *enterprise*, and *industry* to all. The *expression* of that principle, in our Declaration of Independence, was most happy, and fortunate. . . . The assertion of that *principle*, at *that time*, was *the* word, "*fitly spoken*" which has proved an "apple of gold" to us. The *Union*, and the *Constitution*, are the *picture* of *silver*, subsequently framed around it. The picture was made, not to *conceal*, or *destroy* the apple; but to *adorn*, and *preserve* it. The *picture* was made *for* the apple—*not* the apple for the picture."[22]

Lincoln further established the supremacy of the Declaration in November 1863, when he delivered the Gettysburg Address. "Four score and seven years ago," he intoned famously, "our fathers brought forth on this continent, a new nation, conceived in Liberty, and dedicated to the proposition that all men are created equal." Four score and seven? 1776? Our Fathers didn't bring anything forth in 1776. In 1776, our Fathers were getting their hats handed to them by the British (nowhere so conspicuously as in the Battle of Long Island). Our legal charter, the government we live under, was formed in 1787. As Garry Wills and others have pointed out, Lincoln should really have begun his speech with the less mellifluent line: "Three score and sixteen years ago. . . ." But Lincoln was reaching beyond our compromised Constitutional birth to root the Tree of Liberty at the purer headwaters of the Declaration.[23]

In his Annual Message to Congress in 1861, Lincoln made his most explicit statement of how the Declaration was to be implemented. "This is essentially a People's contest," he said of the war at its outset, "a struggle for maintaining in the world, that form, and substance of government, whose leading object is, to elevate the condition of men—to lift artificial weights from all shoulders—to clear the paths of laudable pursuit for all—to afford all, an unfettered start, and a fair chance, in the race of life."[24]

This, according to Lincoln, is all that our politics is supposed to be about. We are *not* a country dedicated to equality of condition (we're not socialists), but we *are* supposed to be dedicated to a genuine equality of opportunity. In this country, everybody is supposed to start from the same line, everyone gets to run as fast as they can. The Constitution, however sacrosanct, is but a frame of silver—a road-map and a set of rules. It was built, not for itself, but to adorn our apple of gold—our destination and our aspiration—the lodestar of our political life: the Declaration of Independence, whose end-logic is a government that lifts artificial weights from *all* shoulders and affords *all* an unfettered start and a fair chance in the race of life.

That Declaration was read on the streets of Boston in 1776. It was read at a women's rights rally in Seneca Falls in 1848. It was quoted at a cemetery in Gettysburg in 1863. It was read on the streets of the African American town of Hamburg, South Carolina, in 1876 just before the Klan murdered the town's leadership. And it was read again in 1963 on the steps of the Lincoln Memorial, when Martin Luther King declared, "I have a dream."

As Lincoln had foretold, there are "two principles that have stood face to face from the beginning of time; and will ever continue to struggle. The one is the common right of humanity and the other [is the] spirit that says, 'You work and toil and earn bread, and I'll eat it.'" America *may be* a place where the most get the richest the quickest, and this is something to be proud of. But it *must be* a place where *all* get an even chance. We do not get to argue whether leveling the playing field or providing a ladder out of poverty is or isn't the "leading object" of government. We do not get to argue whether such projects could or should be left to the market. We made a pact with ourselves in 1776 and its obligations are nonnegotiable, beyond the reach of the marketplace of ideas or money, beyond the reach of democracy or even the Constitution. They are encoded in our DNA, in our birth, in our declaration of independence. All else is debatable.

Bibliographical Essay

AN EXCERPTED CLASSROOM edition of the Lincoln–Douglas debates has never been published. Until now, instructors have been left to DIY their own versions, which litter the Internet by the dozens. This attests at once to the popularity of using the debates in the classroom as well as to the frustration some instructors have felt at the lack of assignable options.

This said, the Lincoln–Douglas debates have been a consistent source of fascination for scholars, although the earliest narrative accounts were sewn into Lincoln biographies. Harry Jaffa came close to a stand-alone study in his evergreen *Crisis of the House Divided: An Interpretation of the Issues in the Lincoln–Douglas Debates* (1959). However, as a political scientist Jaffa was more interested in Lincoln's political philosophy than in the history of the debates themselves. The first historian to give us a narrative treatment was Richard Heckman in his brief and now out-of-print *Lincoln vs. Douglas*, published in 1967 by Public Affairs Press in Washington, D.C. This was followed by amateur historian Saul Sigelschiffer's exhaustive *The American Conscience: The Drama of the Lincoln–Douglas Debates* in 1973, and David Zarefsky's rhetorical analysis in *Lincoln, Douglas, and Slavery: In the Crucible of Public Debate* (1990). The trouble with all of these latter books, as Allen Guelzo has pointed out, is that they tend to focus relentlessly on the debates while ignoring the larger campaigns of which the debates were an integral part. Guelzo rectified this in *Lincoln and Douglas: The Debates That Defined America*, published in Simon & Schuster's "Lincoln Library" series in 2008. Guelzo's deeper contextualization and research certainly informs the headnotes to this volume.

The text of the debates has been published in a variety of forms over the years. Indeed, the first editor to get his volume to market was none other than Abraham Lincoln, whose meticulous scrapbook of newspaper clippings was transcribed and published by the Ohio Republican Party during the 1860 campaign. As soon as he saw it, Douglas fired off an angry note to the publishers, Follett, Foster & Company, to complain of a stacked deck. "Upon the slight examination of your publication which I have been able to make," he said, "I find that Mr. Lincoln's speeches have been revised, corrected and improved" whereas "[my own transcriptions] are imperfect, and in some respects erroneous." Lincoln's version nevertheless became the accepted text until 1953, when Roy Basler's homework for the *Collected Works of Abraham Lincoln* began the process of restoring both men's words to something like their original condition. Hoping to complete such a restoration, Harold Holzer published *The Lincoln-Douglas Debates: The First Complete, Unexpurgated Text* in 2004, which curiously relied on Lincoln's speeches, as captured by a pro-Douglas newspaper, and Douglas's speeches, as captured by a pro-Lincoln paper. The result was an important piece of scholarship and it was certainly fair for being flattering to neither man, but it seemed an overcorrection to many. To be sure, we will never have a perfect transcription of a set of speeches that were given out-of-doors, amid a boisterous crowd, and sometimes in the midst of a downpour. As Douglas himself noted, conditions "made it impossible for the reporters to hear distinctly and report literally." Even so, Rodney Davis and Douglas Wilson's *The Lincoln–Douglas Debates* (Urbana: University of Illinois Press, 2008) has become, and will likely forever be, the ur-text of the debates because it is the only one to use multiple newspaper accounts to triangulate and corroborate the likeliest language each man used at the time.

Notes

1. Stephen Douglas to Joseph O. Glover quoted in Michael Burlingame, *Abraham Lincoln: A Life* (Baltimore: Johns Hopkins University Press, 2008), p. 1343.

2. Allen C. Guelzo, *Lincoln and Douglas: The Debates That Defined America* (New York: Simon & Schuster, 2008), p. 92.

3. Robert Walter Johannsen, *Stephen A. Douglas* (Champaign: University of Illinois Press, 1997), pp. 73, 447; John G. Sotos, *The Physical Lincoln Complete* (CreateSpace Independent Publishing Platform, 2008); Guelzo, *Lincoln and Douglas*, p. 99.

4. Walter Barlow Stevens, *A Reporter's Lincoln* (Lincoln: University of Nebraska Press, 1916), pp. 69–70.

5. Hiram Fuller, *Belle Brittan on a Tour* (New York: Derby & Jackson, 1858), p. 112.

6. Ira Berlin, *Generations of Captivity: A History of African American Slaves* (Cambridge, MA: Harvard University Press, 2009), p. 168.

7. Thomas E. Schott, *Alexander H. Stephens of Georgia: A Biography* (Baton Rouge: Louisiana State University Press, 1996), p. 334.

8. "The Issue Forced Upon Us," *Albany Evening Journal*, March 9, 1857. It should be noted that although Taney wrote for the majority in the *Dred Scott* case, only one other Justice, Peter Daniel, subscribed to the notion of a limitation on congressional power in the territories or the dictum that African Americans could never be citizens. Even so, Lincoln and other Republicans feared that the tide was turning against them and so sounded the alarm.

9. Allen Thorndike Rice, ed., *Reminiscences of Abraham Lincoln by Distinguished Men of His Time* (New York: Harper & Brothers, 1909), p. 575; William H. Herndon and Jesse W. Weik, *Herndon's Life of Lincoln* (Cleveland: World Pub. Co., 1942), pp. 336–337; Joseph Gillespie to William H. Herndon, January 31, 1866, in Douglas L. Wilson and Rodney O. Davis, *Herndon's Informants* (Champaign: University of Illinois Press, 1997), pp. 184–185.

10. Robert Johannsen, *The Frontier, the Union, and Stephen A. Douglas* (Champaign: University of Illinois Press, 1989), p. 98; Guelzo, *Lincoln and Douglas*, p. 102; Johannsen, *Stephen A. Douglas*, pp. 92, 779.

11. Henry Clay Whitney, *Life on the Circuit with Lincoln* (Estes and Lauriat, 1892), p. 115; Wilson and Davis, *Herndon's Informants*, p. 107; Michael Burlingame, ed., *An Oral History of Abraham Lincoln: John G. Nicolay's Interviews and Essays* (Carbondale: Southern Illinois University Press, 2006), p. 20.

12. Abraham Lincoln, "Address before the Young Men's Lyceum of Springfield, Illinois," January 27, 1838, in Roy P. Basler, *The Collected Works of Abraham Lincoln*, vol. 1 (New Brunswick, NJ: Rutgers University Press, 1953), p. 109.

13. Abraham Lincoln, "Speech at Peoria, Illinois," October 16, 1854, in Basler, *Collected Works*, vol. 2, p. 276.

14. Guelzo, *Lincoln and Douglas*, pp. 114–116.

15. Abraham Lincoln to Joseph O. Cunningham, August 22, 1858, in Basler, *Collected Works*, vol. 3; Lyman Trumbull to Abraham Lincoln, August 24, 1858, in *Abraham Lincoln Papers*, Library of Congress (hereafter *Lincoln Papers*); Henry C. Whitney to Abraham Lincoln, August 26, 1858, *Lincoln Papers*.

16. Lyman Trumbull to Abraham Lincoln, September 14, 1858, *Lincoln Papers*; Guelzo, *Lincoln and Douglas*, p. 173.

17. Guelzo, *Lincoln and Douglas*, p. 186; Sydney Spring to Abraham Lincoln, September 8, 1858, *Lincoln Papers*.

18. David Davis to Abraham Lincoln, November 7, 1858, *Lincoln Papers*; Norman B. Judd to Abraham Lincoln, November 15, 1858, *Lincoln Papers*; Henry P. Bromwell to Abraham Lincoln, November 5, 1858, *Lincoln Papers*; Abraham Lincoln to Norman B. Judd, November 15, 1858, *Lincoln Papers*.

19. Abraham Lincoln to Albert Hodges, April 4, 1864, in Basler, ed., *Collected Works*, vol. 7, p. 281; Abraham Lincoln, "Speech to One Hundred Fortieth Indiana Regiment," March 18, 1865, in Basler, ed., *Collected Works*, vol. 8, p. 360.

20. Frederick Douglass in Rice, ed., *Reminiscences of Abraham Lincoln*, p. 195.

21. Henry Hughes (writing as "St. Henry"), "Re-opening of the African Labor Supply—Number Seven—Wealth Argument," Jackson *Semi-Weekly Mississippian*, October 4, 1859; see also Douglas Ambrose, *Henry Hughes and Proslavery Thought in the Old South* (Baton Rouge: Louisiana State University Press, 1996).

22. Abraham Lincoln, "Fragment on the Constitution and the Union," c. January 1861 in Basler, ed., *Collected Works*, vol. 4, p. 169.

23. Garry Wills, *Lincoln at Gettysburg: The Words That Remade America* (New York: Simon & Schuster, 1992).

24. Abraham Lincoln, "Message to Congress in Special Session," July 4, 1861, in Basler, ed., *Collected Works*, vol. 4, p. 421.

Credits

MAPS

Map Introduction-1:

George Chakvetadze

Map Epilogue-1:

George Chakvetadze

Index

Page numbers in *italics* indicate the reference is in one of the speeches.

abolition, 16, 26–27, 42,
African-American citizenship, 48
Alton, IL, 75
Associated Press, 3

Baldwin, Abraham, 91
"Black Republicans," 30
Blount, William, 90
Booth, John Wilkes, 47
Breckenridge, John C., 9
Breese, Sidney, 36
Bromwell, Henry, 84
Brooks, Preston, 38
Brown, John, 93
Buchanan, James, 8, 73

Cass, Lewis, 8, 36,
Charleston, IL, 3, 45, 56
Chase, Salmon P., 16, 36
Charleston, IL, 45
Chicago, IL, 1, 51, 55, 56
Clay, Henry, 27, 47, 63, 64
Cobb, Howell, 8
colonization, 64
Crittenden, John Jordan, 83
Crittenden-Montgomery Bill, 31
Cuba, 39

Davis, David, 83
Declaration of Independence, 47–48, 55, 56–58, 64, 78, 99
Democratic Party, 15–16, 59, 69, 77
Dickey, Theophilus, 83
disunion, 24, 79
Douglas, Stephen A.: and state sovereignty, 23–24; appearance of, 4; early career of, 5; Freeport Doctrine of, 25–26, 28–29, 35, 40; on Fugitive Slave Law, 32; on his own

background, 42; on Lincoln's background, 19; on Lincoln's inconsistencies, 56, 57–58; on Lincoln's stance against Mexican-American War, 20, 78; racial attitudes of, 30, 45, 48, 55–56, 58; on the Supreme Court, 29–30; on territorial acquisition and U.S. expansion, 30, 39; on Toombs bill, 50; opinion of Lincoln of, 9; rhetorical style of, 9–10; speech at Alton, IL, of, 75–81; speech at Charleston, IL of, 47–53; speech at Columbus, OH of, 85–89; speech at Freeport, IL of, 26–34; speech at Galesburg, IL, 55–65; speech at Jonesboro, IL of, 35–43; speech at Ottawa, IL of, 15–24; speech at Quincy, IL, of, 70–74; title of "Judge" of, 72
Dred Scott v. Sanford, 9, 29, 39, 47, 48, 59, 61, 71, 73, 78
Douglass, Frederick, 16, 30, 36, 98

Election of 1860, 84
Euclid, 52

Few, William, 90
Fitzsimmons, Thomas, 90
Founding Fathers, 21, 24, 38–39, 43, 53, 74, 89–92
Floyd, John, 8
Freeport, IL, 25, 36,
Fremont, John C., 15
Fugitive Slave Law, 16, 32

Galesburg, IL, 55
Garrison, William Lloyd, 98
gerrymandering, 84
Giddings, Joshua, 16, 36,

Hannibal, MO, 67
Harper's Ferry, 93
Hughes, Henry, 98